English G 21

Grammar and Skills A3/4

English G 21

Grammar and Skills 3/4
zu den Bänden 3 und 4
der Ausgabe A für Gymnasien

Im Auftrag des Verlages herausgegeben von
Prof. Hellmut Schwarz, Mannheim

Erarbeitet von
Ursula Fleischhauer, Hannover
Uwe Tröger, Hannover,
und
Dr. Philip Devlin, Berlin (Grammar),
Birgit Ohmsieder, Berlin (Skills),
Joachim Blombach, Herford (Skills),
Helmut Dengler, Limbach (Skills),
Sabine Tudan, Erfurt (Skills)

unter Mitarbeit von
Birgit Heinemann, Neu-Wulmstorf,
Joachim Sauer, Ostseebad Rerik,
Andreas Sedlatschek, Esslingen am Neckar
sowie
Jennifer Seidl, München

Illustration
Roland Beier, Berlin

Fotos
Marion Schönenberger, Berlin (S. 76)

Titelbild
www.fotolia.de (Wegweiser [M]: endrille)

Umschlaggestaltung
Klein & Halm Grafikdesign, Berlin

Layoutkonzept
Aksinia Raphael, Korinna Wilkes

Technische Umsetzung
Stephan Hilleckenbach, Berlin;
Ina Hillmann

www.cornelsen.de
www.EnglishG.de
Dieses Werk berücksichtigt die Regeln der reformierten Rechtschreibung und Zeichensetzung.

1. Auflage, 1. Druck 2009

Alle Drucke dieser Auflage sind inhaltlich unverändert und können im Unterricht nebeneinander verwendet werden.

Druck: CS-Druck CornelsenStürtz, Berlin

ISBN 978-3-06-031025-8

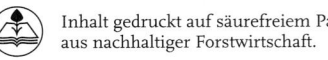
Inhalt gedruckt auf säurefreiem Papier aus nachhaltiger Forstwirtschaft.

Was enthält dieses Heft?

Wie du schon am Titel sehen kannst, besteht dieses Heft aus zwei Teilen:
- einem **Grammar**-Teil (S. 6–73)
- einem **Skills**-Teil (S. 74–94).

Im **Grammar**-Teil wird der Grammatikstoff der Klassen 7 und 8 zusammengefasst und erklärt. Außerdem werden die wesentlichen grammatischen Themen der Klassen 5 und 6 wiederholt.

Im **Skills**-Teil werden wichtige Lern- und Arbeitstechniken vorgestellt und erläutert.

 Lies bitte zuerst die Hinweise auf dieser Seite, damit du weißt, wie du am besten mit diesem Heft arbeitest.

Wie findest du, was du suchst?

1. Du kannst in den Inhaltsverzeichnissen nachschlagen:

- Auf den **Seiten 4–5** findest du das Inhaltsverzeichnis für den **Grammar**-Teil. Dort kannst du nachschlagen, wenn du ein bestimmtes grammatisches Kapitel suchst.

- Auf **Seite 74** findest du das Inhaltsverzeichnis für den **Skills**-Teil. Dort kannst du nachschlagen, wenn du Informationen zu einer bestimmten Lern- oder Arbeitstechnik suchst.

2. Du kannst im **Stichwortregister** auf den **Seiten 95–97** nachschlagen. Dort sind alle grammatischen Strukturen und auch einzelne wichtige englische und deutsche Wörter **alphabetisch** aufgelistet, und du siehst sofort, in welchen Abschnitten des Grammar-Teils du etwas zu deinem gesuchten Begriff findest.

Was bedeuten die Zeichen und Abkürzungen?

Die Ziffern bei den Abschnitts-Überschriften sagen dir, wo dieses Thema in den Bänden 3 und 4 des Lehrwerks *English G 21*, Ausgabe A, behandelt wird:

3 : 2 / 4 : 1	bedeutet Band 3, Unit 2 und Band 4, Unit 1

▶ *The future: 19–22*
▶ *Handouts (p. 79)*
Der Pfeil ▶ verweist auf andere Abschnitte, in denen du weitere Informationen zum gerade behandelten Thema findest.

 Hier stehen Hinweise, die du besonders beachten solltest, um Fehler zu vermeiden.

 Das **K** steht für „Kontrast". Du findest es im Grammar-Teil immer dort, wo auf wichtige Unterschiede zwischen dem Englischen und dem Deutschen hingewiesen wird.

Additional information

Abschnitte mit der Überschrift „Additional information" enthalten Grammatik, die du nicht selbst anwenden können musst.
Du solltest aber verstehen, was dort erläutert wird, damit du keine Schwierigkeiten mit Texten hast, in denen diese Grammatik vorkommt.

 *Am Ende der Abschnitte stehen oft kleine Aufgaben. Mit diesen Aufgaben kannst du überprüfen, ob du alles richtig verstanden hast.*
Die Lösungen stehen auf den Seiten 71–73 (Grammar) und 92–94 (Skills).

Inhalt

Grammar

Word order (Wortstellung)

1 Positive statements (Bejahte Aussagesätze)

1	**Subject**	**Verb***		
	Asif	is working.		
2	**Subject**	**Verb**	**Adverbial**	
	Katrina	lives	in Scotland.	
3	**Subject**	**Verb**	**Complement***	
	Latisha	was	happy.	
4	**Subject**	**Verb**	**Object**	
	My sister	can play	the piano.	
5	**Subject**	**Verb**	**Object**	**Adverbial**
	The Clarks	have bought	a house	in Wales.

K 1 We're going to produce a music magazine.
Wir werden eine Musikzeitschrift produzieren.

2 Latisha often plays football at the weekends.
Latisha spielt am Wochenende oft Fußball.

3 After lunch they took the Tube to Green Park.
Nach dem Essen nahmen sie die U-Bahn nach Green Park.

4 When I got to the station, the train had already left.
Als ich am Bahnhof ankam, war der Zug schon abgefahren.

Wortstellung:
S – V – O, wie in S**traßen-**V**erkehrs-**O**rdnung!**

2 Negative statements (Verneinte Aussagesätze)

Subject	Verb		Object
	Auxiliary + **not**	Main verb	
Katrina	does**n't**	play	the piano.
Fiona	ca**n't**	speak	German.
I	have**n't**	done	my homework.

Ein Satz besteht aus mindestens zwei Satzgliedern: **Subjekt** und **Prädikat** – englisch: *subject* (S) und *verb** (V).

Weitere Satzglieder können hinzutreten:
– eine **adverbiale Bestimmung** *(adverbial)* (Satz 2)
– eine **Ergänzung** *(complement**)* (Satz 3)
– ein **Objekt** (O) *(object)* (Satz 4).

! Die wichtigste Wortstellungsregel im Englischen ist S – V – O.
Beachte dabei, dass V und O unzertrennlich sind und nie durch ein anderes Satzglied voneinander getrennt werden dürfen.

! **Anders als im Deutschen**
– werden die Teile des Prädikats nie durch das Objekt voneinander getrennt (Satz 1),

– werden Prädikat und Objekt (**V** und **O**) nicht durch Adverbien oder Zeitangaben voneinander getrennt (Satz 2),

– ist die Wortstellung auch dann **S – V – ...**, wenn der Satz mit einer adverbialen Bestimmung *(After lunch; When I got to the station)* beginnt (Sätze 3, 4).

Auch in verneinten Aussagesätzen ist die Wortstellung **S – V – O**.

* *Das Wort **verb** bezeichnet im Englischen nicht nur die Wortart „Verb", sondern auch das Satzglied „Prädikat".*

** *Ein Adjektiv oder Nomen, das nach einer Form von* (to) *be steht, wird als **Ergänzung zum Subjekt** (subject complement) bezeichnet.*

3 Questions (Fragesätze)

3.1 Yes/No questions (Entscheidungsfragen)

Auxiliary	Subject	Main verb	Object / Adverbial	
Is	**Asif**	working?		
Can	**you**	speak	Spanish?	
Have	**they**	bought	a house	yet?
Does	**Katrina**	live	in Wales?	

Entscheidungsfragen beginnen <u>immer</u> mit einem **Hilfsverb** *(auxiliary)*.
Die Wortstellung ist also:
Auxiliary – S – V – … .

3.2 Questions with question words (Fragen mit Fragewörtern)

Question word	Auxiliary	Subject	Main verb	Object / Adverbial
What	is	**Asif**	doing?	
Where	does	**Katrina**	live?	
Why	can't	**I**	have	a pet?
When	are	**you**	going to do	your homework?
Who	did	**Robert**	meet	in Birmingham?

Auch in Fragen, die mit einem Fragewort beginnen, steht ein **Hilfsverb** vor dem Subjekt. Die Wortstellung ist also:
Question word – auxiliary – S – V – … .

! **Ausnahmen:**
Fragen nach dem Subjekt
▶ *Fragen nach dem Subjekt: 3.3*

K
What **are** you **waiting** for?	Worauf **wartest** du?
Who **did** you **talk** to?	Mit wem **hast** du **geredet**?
Where **do** you **come** from?	Woher **kommst** du?

! Eine Präposition bleibt im Englischen auch in der Frage hinter dem Verb stehen (und ist meist das letzte Wort der Frage).

3.3 Subject questions (Fragen nach dem Subjekt)

!
Statement	Subject question	Object question
Jack loves Ella.	Who loves Ella?	Who does Jack love?
Jack liebt Ella.	Wer liebt Ella?	Wen liebt Jack?
Hull beat Arsenal.	Which team won?	Which team did Hull beat?
Hull schlug Arsenal.	Welches Team siegte?	Welches Team schlug Hull?
	(Wer? – *Antwort:* Hull)	(Wen? – *Antwort:* Arsenal)

- Fragen nach dem **Subjekt** („**Wer oder was?**") werden <u>ohne</u> das Hilfsverb *do/does/did* gebildet.

- Fragen nach dem **Objekt** („**Wen/Wem oder was?**") werden <u>mit</u> Hilfsverb *do/does* (im *simple present*) bzw. *did* (im *simple past*) gebildet.

1 What **happened** when Luke opened the door?
Was geschah, als Luke die Tür öffnete?
2 What did Luke **see** when he opened the door?
Was sah Luke, als er die Tür öffnete?

1 Whose grandma **came** to England from Trinidad?
Wessen Oma („Wer?") kam aus Trinidad nach England?
2 Whose parents did Asif **meet** in London?
Wessen Eltern („Wen?") hat Asif in London getroffen?

(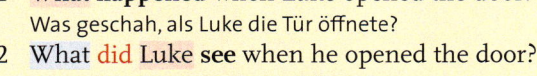 = subject   –   = object)

Weitere Beispiele für *subject questions* (1) und *object questions* (2) stehen links.

 Fragen nach dem Subjekt <u>ohne</u> *do/does/did*!

Bilde zwei Fragen zu jedem Satz.

1 Katrina met Latisha at the festival in Birmingham.

A (Wer traf Latisha ...?) Who ... at the festival?
B (Wen traf Katrina ...?) Who ... at the festival?

2 Robert wants to keep in touch with Asif.

A (Wer ...?) Who ...?
B (Mit wem ...?) Who ...?

3 Every morning Mrs McFadden takes Katrina to the ferry.

A (Wer ...?) Who ... every morning?
B (Wen ...?) Who ... every morning?

4 Subordinate clauses (Nebensätze)

Hauptsatz	Nebensatz (Subordinate clause)		
	Subject	**V**erb	**O**bject
Dad will help you	if	you	ask	him.
I like museums	because	I	like	paintings.
Latisha says	that	she	loves	ManU.
They stopped	when	they	saw	me.
I don't know	where	I	put	my keys.

Anders als im Deutschen gilt die Wortstellungsregel **S – V – O** auch für Nebensätze.

Vergleiche: **S   V   O**
... if you **ask him**.
... wenn du **ihn fragst**.

5 Sentences with two objects (Sätze mit zwei Objekten)

4:1

	Indirect object	Direct object
Caitlin **showed**	Ryan	some New York sights.
I'll **send**	you	a postcard.
Mum **bought**	me	a souvenir.
Dad **told**	us	a great story.

**Person vor Sache –
wie im Alphabet: *p* vor *s*.**

Wie im Deutschen gibt es im Englischen Verben, nach denen zwei Objekte stehen können:
– ein **indirektes Objekt** (meist eine **Person**, daher auch **Personenobjekt** genannt),
– ein **direktes Objekt** (meist eine **Sache**, daher auch **Sachobjekt** genannt).

Die normale Wortstellung ist **Person vor Sache**:
*(to) give/show/tell **somebody something**
jemandem etwas geben/zeigen/erzählen.*

Here's a nice postcard. Let's **send** it to Mum and Dad. Katrina bought some CDs and **showed** them to Latisha. That's a great poster, isn't it? I **bought** it for my sister.

Ist das **Sachobjekt** ein **Pronomen** *(it, them)*, steht es **direkt hinter dem Verb**.
Das **Personenobjekt** wird dann mit **to** angeschlossen. (Bei den Verben *buy, cook, get, make, order* mit **for**).

Let's **write** a postcard to our aunt and uncle in the USA. I **bought** that poster for my sister (not for you).

Die Wortstellung **Sachobjekt – to/for – Personenobjekt** gilt auch dann, wenn
● das Personenobjekt sehr lang ist
● das Personenobjekt besonders betont werden soll.

Now **describe** the picture to your partner.
Please **explain** to us what happened.
Present your ideas to the class.
I **didn't say** anything to the others.

! Bei einigen Verben wird das Personenobjekt immer mit *to* angehängt. Zu diesen Verben gehören *describe, explain, introduce, present, report, say.*

Bilde Sätze. Achte auf die richtige Stellung der Objekte.

1 Have you got my ruler? I ... (give / you / it) yesterday.
2 Didn't Mum say she wanted to ... (make / me / a cake)? Where is it?
– No, no. Mum said she wanted ... (make / Dad / a cake), not for you!
3 Could you ... (explain / the team / the problem), please?

6 Adverbs and adverbial phrases (Adverbien und Adverbialbestimmungen)

front-position		mid-position		end-position
↓		↓		↓
adverb	**subject (+ auxiliary)**	adverb	**main verb (+ object)**	adverb

Adverbien und Adverbialbestimmungen können an verschiedenen Stellen im Satz stehen.

6.1 Front-position

Suddenly **the car** stopped and two men got out.

Of course **you** can borrow my bike.

Luckily **we** had our anoraks with us.

Vor dem Subjekt – also in *front-position* – stehen in der Regel Adverbien, die sich auf den ganzen Satz beziehen (sogenannte **Satzadverbien**).
Beispiele: *perhaps, maybe, suddenly, luckily, finally, then, of course, in fact, at first, ...*

6.2 Mid-position

1 My brother **is** always late.
It was only 11, but we **were** already hungry.

2 I often **make** breakfast on Sundays.
They didn't have a map and soon **got** lost.

3 Emma **doesn't** usually take the bus to school.
Your uncle **has** just phoned.
That story **will** never be forgotten.

Mid-position haben gewöhnlich **Adverbien** wie *already, always, ever, just, never, often, sometimes, soon, usually,* die eine **unbestimmte Zeit oder Häufigkeit** beschreiben. Sie stehen
■ **nach *am/are/is*** und ***was/were*** (1)
■ direkt **vor dem Vollverb** (im *simple present* und *simple past*) (2)
■ **nach dem (ersten) Hilfsverb** (3).

Have you been here before? (schon mal)
Have you cleaned the kitchen yet? (schon)
The play hasn't started yet. (noch nicht)

! Beachte:
■ ***before*** und ***yet*** stehen **am Satzende**.

Sometimes we have a really big breakfast on Sundays.
Often we're so full that we don't eat lunch!

■ ***sometimes*** und ***often*** können auch *front-position* haben.

K I always make the same mistakes.
Ich mache immer dieselben Fehler.

! Anders als im Deutschen dürfen Adverbien der unbestimmten Zeit oder Häufigkeit **nicht zwischen Prädikat und Objekt** stehen.

6.3 **End-position**

1 The woman **shouted** angrily.
My cousin speaks **Spanish** well.

2 Can we go and **play** outside.
I first met **my girlfriend** at a disco.

3 Sally sold **her motorbike** yesterday.
My grandmother **died** two years ago.

	Art u. Weise	Ort	Zeit
Alison is flying		to New York	tomorrow.
Philip sang	well	at the party	last night.

K Every Saturday morning my father does the shopping.
Jeden Samstagmorgen erledigt mein Vater die Einkäufe.

K He closed the door quietly.
Er schloss leise die Tür.

We're going to buy a new car next month.
Wir kaufen nächsten Monat ein neues Auto.

 Adverbien und Adverbial-
bestimmungen <u>nie</u> zwischen
Prädikat und Objekt!

6.4 **Adverbs of degree (Gradadverbien)**

Your new camera looks very **expensive**.
My parents are quite **strict** / too **strict**.
Do you really **believe** you'll be famous one day?

Nach dem Vollverb bzw. nach dem Objekt
– also in *end-position* – stehen in der Regel

- **Adverbien der Art und Weise** (*angrily, well*) (1)

- **Adverbien und Adverbialbestimmungen des Ortes** (*outside; at a disco*) (2)

- **Adverbien und Adverbialbestimmungen der Zeit** (*yesterday; two years ago*) (3).

Wenn verschiedene Adverbien bzw. Adverbialbestimmungen am Satzende zusammenkommen, dann gilt gewöhnlich die Reihenfolge **Art und Weise – Ort – Zeit** (wie im Alphabet: *a* vor *o* vor *z*).

! Zeitangaben können auch *front-position* haben. Anders als im Deutschen bleibt die Wortstellung dann trotzdem **S – V – O**.

! Anders als im Deutschen dürfen Adverbien der Art und Weise und Orts- und Zeitangaben **nicht zwischen Prädikat und Objekt** stehen.

Die Gradadverbien *very, quite, too* (= „zu"), *really* stehen direkt vor dem Wort, auf das sie sich beziehen.

Setze die Adverbien und Adverbialbestimmungen an die richtigen Stellen und bilde sinnvolle Sätze.

1 They found out why Jack had shouted. (soon – angrily)
2 'We can see the village from this tree,' he said and climbed it. (perhaps – carefully)
3 I'm nervous before a test. (often)   But I do well in the end. (usually – quite)
4 I've wanted to have a picnic. (always – in Central Park – on a warm summer evening)

The verb (Das Verb)

7 Types of verbs (Verbarten)

- (to) **ask**, (to) **give**, (to) **go**, (to) **love**, (to) **swim**, (to) **try**, ...
- **be, do, have**
- **can, could, may, might, must, mustn't, needn't, shall, should, will, would**

Englische Verben lassen sich in drei Gruppen einteilen:

- **Vollverben** (full verbs) ► 7.1 / Zeitformen: 8
- die drei Verben **be, do, have**, die als **Voll-** oder **Hilfsverb** verwendet werden ► 7.2
- **modale Hilfsverben** (modal auxiliaries / modals). ► 23 / will-future: 20

7.1 Full verbs (Vollverben)

I love New York.
Ryan went to New York and visited his cousin.

Vollverben können **allein** – d.h. ohne ein Hilfsverb – im Satz auftreten.

Von jedem englischen Vollverb gibt es **fünf Formen**.

■ **Infinitiv** (infinitive)	(to) **ask**, (to) **give**, (to) **swim**, (to) **try**
■ **-s-Form** für die 3. Person Singular des *simple present*	(he/she/it) ask**s**, give**s**, swim**s**, trie**s**
■ **-ing-Form**	ask**ing**, giv**ing**, swimm**ing**, try**ing**
■ **Simple past-Form**	ask**ed**, **gave**, **swam**, **tried**
■ **Partizip Perfekt** (past participle)	ask**ed**, **given**, **swum**, **tried**

! **Unregelmäßige Verben** wie *give* und *swim* haben eigene *simple past-* und *past participle*-Formen.
► Unregelmäßige Verben: 63

7.2 be, do, have

Die Verben **be**, **do** und **have** können **Voll- oder Hilfsverb** sein.

! **be** als Vollverb wird in Fragen und Verneinungen **nicht** mit dem Hilfsverb *do* umschrieben.

Vollverb (Full verb)

be	I'm Lily. I'm in Mr Parker's class. I wasn't in his class last year. Were you in his class?
do	My brother and I do a lot of sport. Do you do a lot of sport? Have you done your homework?
have	We usually have dinner at seven o'clock. Our neighbours don't have any pets. Did you have a good time in Spain?

Als **Hilfsverben** dienen *be*, *do* und **have** zur Bildung bestimmter Zeitformen der Vollverben.

Hilfsverb (Auxiliary verb)

be	Jonathan is **repairing** his bike. My skates were **made** in the USA.
do	Does she **live** here? – I don't **know**. Don't **worry**, I didn't **forget** your birthday.
have	Pamela has just **phoned**. It was too late. The last bus had **left**.

► Kurzformen: 62

8   The tenses of the full verbs
(Die Zeitformen der Vollverben)

8.1   Tense and time
(Grammatische Zeit und wirkliche Zeit)

Tense (Zeitform)	Time (wirkliche Zeit)		
present present perfect past past perfect future future perfect	the past	the present	the future

Wenn man von **„Zeit"** spricht, muss man zwischen der **grammatischen Zeit(form)** und der **wirklichen Zeit** unterscheiden.

- The next bus leaves **in 15 minutes.**   **Simple present** mit
  Der nächste Bus fährt in 15 Minuten.   Bezug auf die **Zukunft**

- If I met Jill **tomorrow,** ...   **Simple past** mit Bezug
  Wenn ich Jill morgen träfe/   auf die **Zukunft**
  treffen würde, ...

Grammatische Zeitformen können sich auf verschiedene Zeiten in der Wirklichkeit beziehen. *Simple present* und *simple past* beziehen sich in den Beispielen links nicht auf die Gegenwart bzw. die Vergangenheit, sondern auf die Zukunft.

K   I've known Jill for 8 years.   Present perfect
Ich kenne Jill seit 8 Jahren.   Präsens

Wait. I'll help you.   *will*-future
Warte. Ich helfe dir.   Präsens

!   Die Zeitformen werden im Englischen und im Deutschen oft unterschiedlich verwendet.

8.2   Simple form and progressive form
(Einfache Form und Verlaufsform)

Tense	Simple form	Progressive form
present	sing(s)	am/are/is singing
present perfect	have/has sung	have/has been singing
past	sang	was/were singing
past perfect	had sung	had been singing
will-future	will sing	will be singing

Im Englischen gibt es neben der **einfachen Form** des Verbs auch noch eine sogenannte **Verlaufsform** *(progressive form).*

Die **Verlaufsform** drückt aus, dass eine Handlung **im Verlauf**, also **noch nicht abgeschlossen** ist (bzw. war).

Daniel is writing an essay.
Daniel schreibt (gerade) einen Aufsatz.

Daniel has been doing his homework all afternoon.
Daniel ist schon den ganzen Nachmittag dabei, seine Hausaufgaben zu machen. *(Er ist noch nicht fertig.)*

Daniel was doing his homework when suddenly his
computer crashed.
Daniel machte (gerade) seine Hausaufgaben, ...

!   Im Deutschen gibt es keine Verlaufsform. Aber manchmal sagt man „Ich **bin gerade dabei**, meine Hausaufgaben zu machen", um zum Ausdruck zu bringen, dass etwas noch im Gange und noch nicht abgeschlossen ist.

**8.3 The tenses – overview
(Die Zeitformen – Übersicht)**

Die folgende Übersicht enthält Langformen
(I will not ask).
Beim Sprechen und in persönlichen Briefen
werden meist Kurzformen verwendet
(I won't ask). ▶ *Kurzformen: 62*

		Active	**Passive** ▶ *24*
Present	**Simple present** ▶ *10*	I ask I do not ask Do I ask?	I am asked I am not asked Am I asked?
	Present progressive ▶ *11*	I am asking I am not asking Am I asking?	
Past	**Simple past** ▶ *13*	I asked I did not ask Did I ask?	I was asked I was not asked Was I asked?
	Past progressive ▶ *14*	I was asking I was not asking Was I asking?	
Present perfect	**Present perfect (simple)** ▶ *15*	I have asked I have not asked Have I asked?	I have been asked I have not been asked Have I been asked?
	Present perfect progressive ▶ *16*	I have been asking I have not been asking Have I been asking?	
Past perfect	**Past perfect (simple)** ▶ *17*	I had asked I had not asked Had I asked?	I had been asked I had not been asked Had I been asked?
	Past perfect progressive ▶ *18*	I had been asking I had not been asking Had I been asking?	
Future	***will*-future** ▶ *20*	I will ask I will not ask Will I ask?	I will be asked I will not be asked Will I be asked?
	***going to*-future** ▶ *21*	I am going to ask I am not going to ask Am I going to ask?	I am going to be asked I am not going to be asked Am I going to be asked?
Future perfect	**Future perfect** ▶ *22*	I will have asked I will not have asked Will I have asked?	

9 The present – in a nutshell
(Die Gegenwart – das Wichtigste in Kürze)

Simple present

Ella goes to school by bike. Her brother usually takes the bus. They never walk, but their parents sometimes take them by car.

The Blakes live in Chester. Mrs Blake works for a computer company. Mr Blake looks after their children. At the weekends Mrs Blake plays the piano and writes short stories.

▶ Simple present: 10

■ Mit dem *simple present* drückt man aus, dass etwas **wiederholt, regelmäßig, immer** oder **nie** geschieht.

Das *simple present* wird daher z.B. verwendet, um über **Hobbys, Berufe** und **Dauerzustände** zu sprechen.

Present progressive

We can't come to the beach with you. I'm still working on my essay for tomorrow, Owen is trying to repair his bike, and Mum is practising the piano.

Olivia has got a holiday job: she's working as a waitress in a small café in Bristol. She's sharing a room with another waitress while she's there.

▶ Present progressive: 11

■ Mit dem *present progressive* drückt man aus, dass **jemand gerade dabei ist**, etwas zu tun, oder dass etwas **gerade im Gange** und **noch nicht abgeschlossen** ist.

Das *present progressive* wird daher auch für **vorübergehende Zustände** verwendet.

Simple present	Present progressive

Jack Whitlam works as an architect.	He's working at his desk at the moment.

Simple present *oder* **present progressive?**

1 My sister (usually – **have**) milk for breakfast, but this morning she (**drink**) tea.
2 At the weekend we (often – **go**) to Camden Lock Market with our friends.
3 Normally I (**get up**) at seven o'clock, but this week I (**get up**) later because there's no school.
4 We (usually – **play**) tennis at weekends, but this weekend we (**visit**) friends in Bath.
5 *(On the phone)* 'I can't talk to you right now. I (just – **wash**) my hair.'

10 The simple present
(Die einfache Form der Gegenwart)

10.1 Form (Form)

I/You **play**	I/You **don't play**	**Do**	I/you	**play?**
He/She/It **plays**	He/She/It **doesn't play**	**Does**	he/she/it	**play?**
We/You/They **play**	We/You/They **don't play**	**Do**	we/you/they	**play?**

▶ *Kurzformen: 62*

! (to) try – **he/she/it** tries   (to) copy – **he/she/it** copies

He, she, it –
das „s" muss mit.

- Das *simple present* hat die Form des Infinitivs. Nur bei der 3. Person Singular *(he/she/it)* wird **-(e)s** angehängt.

- **Verneinte Sätze** bildet man mit **don't** bzw. **doesn't**.

- **Fragen** bildet man mit **do** bzw. **does**.

10.2 Use (Gebrauch)

I **often** ride my bike to school.
We go camping **every summer**.

Das *simple present* wird verwendet,

- um auszudrücken, dass etwas **wiederholt** (regelmäßig, immer, jeden Tag, oft, ...) oder **nie** geschieht. In *simple present*-Sätzen stehen oft die Signalwörter *always, often, sometimes, usually, never* oder Zeitangaben wie *every summer, on Fridays, at weekends*, ...

Katrina plays the fiddle.
Mrs Kent works in an office. She speaks four languages.

- wenn man über Hobbys, Berufe und Fähigkeiten spricht.

When you mix blue and yellow you get green.
Children all over the world play football.

- wenn man sagen will, dass etwas immer oder überall der Fall ist.

She goes into the room, pulls open the curtains and looks out of the window.
First you go along Elm Street, then you turn left and cross the bridge. After the bridge you turn right. ...

- um mehrere **aufeinanderfolgende Handlungen** zu beschreiben (oft in Erzählungen und in Gebrauchsanweisungen oder Auskünften).

The author describes a journey to Wales that goes terribly wrong.
What does the text say about his parents?

- wenn man über einen Text, einen Film, ein Theaterstück spricht.

The film starts at 8 o'clock.
When does the next train to Liverpool leave?
The club meets in an hour, so we'll have to hurry

▶ *The future: 19–22*

Das *simple present* wird auch benutzt um auszudrücken, dass etwas **Zukünftiges** durch einen **Fahrplan**, ein **Programm**, einen **Kalender** oder Ähnliches festgelegt ist. (Diese Verwendung des *simple present* wird manchmal *timetable future* genannt.)

11 The present progressive
(Die Verlaufsform der Gegenwart)

11.1 Form (Form)

I'm **playing**	I'm **not** playing	**Am** I **playing?**
You're **playing**	You **aren't** playing	**Are** you **playing?**
He's/She's/It's **playing**	He/She/It **isn't** playing	**Is** he/she/it **playing?**
We're **playing**	We **aren't** playing	**Are** we **playing?**
You're **playing**	You **aren't** playing	**Are** you **playing?**
They're **playing**	They **aren't** playing	**Are** they **playing?**

▶ *Kurzformen: 62*

❗ (to) mak**e**, (to) giv**e**, ... + **-ing** → making, giving, ...
(to) ru**n**, (to) dro**p**, ... + **-ing** → ru**nn**ing, dro**pp**ing, ...

Das *present progressive* wird mit **am/are/is** + **-ing form** gebildet.

11.2 Use (Gebrauch)

Jaden is in the park with Cole. They're playing football.
What are you doing? – I'm trying to repair the CD player.

I'm busy, David. I'm helping Dad to tidy up the kitchen.

My sister usually looks after our dog but she's ill,
so I'm feeding Fluffy this week.

Mum I'm meeting some friends in town **next Friday**,
so Dad is picking you up from school.

▶ *The future: 19–22*

Das *present progressive* wird verwendet,

- um auszudrücken, dass **jemand gerade etwas tut** oder dass **etwas noch im Gange** und **noch nicht abgeschlossen** ist. **Signalwörter:** *now, at the moment, just* („gerade"), *still* („noch").

  ❗ Die Handlung, um die es geht, kann für einen Augenblick unterbrochen sein – z.B. durch ein Telefonat. Wichtig ist, dass sie noch nicht abgeschlossen ist.

- wenn man sagen will, dass etwas **nur vorübergehend der Fall** ist.

Das *present progressive* wird auch benutzt, wenn etwas **für die Zukunft fest geplant** oder **fest verabredet** ist *(diary future)*. Durch eine Zeitangabe oder aus dem Zusammenhang muss klar sein, dass es sich um etwas Zukünftiges handelt.

agree	übereinstimmen	**mean**	bedeuten
believe	glauben	**need**	brauchen
belong	gehören	**notice**	bemerken
cost	kosten	**own**	besitzen
hate	hassen	**seem**	*(zu sein/zu tun)* scheinen
hear	hören	**smell**	riechen, stinken
like	mögen	**sound**	klingen
love	lieben	**taste**	schmecken

❗ Verben, die keine Tätigkeiten beschreiben *(know, want, ...)* werden normalerweise nicht in der *progressive form* verwendet. Weitere Beispiele für solche Verben stehen links.

12 **The past – in a nutshell**
(Die Vergangenheit – das Wichtigste in Kürze) 3: 4 / 4: 5

12.1 **Simple past, past progressive**

Simple past

Robert went to Ashley's party last Friday.
Sam was invited too, but he wasn't allowed to go.
He had to stay at home.

Robert gave Ashley a DVD.
Robert hat Ashley eine DVD geschenkt.

▶ *Simple past: 13*

Past progressive

The other guests were laughing and talking
when Robert arrived. Robert put on some music,
and soon everybody was dancing.

▶ *Past progressive: 14*

- Mit dem *simple past* beschreibt man,
was **zu einem bestimmten Zeitpunkt in
der Vergangenheit** geschah.

  ! Im Deutschen steht oft das Perfekt,
  wo im Englischen das *simple past*
  stehen muss.

- Mit dem *past progressive* sagt man, dass
etwas zu einem bestimmten Zeitpunkt
in der Vergangenheit **im Gange** und
noch nicht abgeschlossen war.

12.2 **Present perfect, present perfect progressive**

Present perfect

The DJ has set up his equipment. The dancing
can begin.

I've been an *Interpol* fan since the band's first hit.
Ich bin *Interpol*-Fan seit dem ersten Hit der Band.

▶ *Present perfect: 15*

Present perfect progressive

Robert has been DJing at Ashley's party for over
three hours now.
Robert legt seit über drei Stunden auf Ashleys Party auf.

▶ *Present perfect progressive: 16*

Beide Formen des **present perfect** haben
mit Vergangenheit <u>und</u> Gegenwart zu tun:

- Mit dem *present perfect* sagt man,
  – dass **etwas geschehen** ist. Wann das
    war, interessiert nicht, aber oft hat
    das Geschehen Auswirkungen auf die
    Gegenwart oder Zukunft.
  – dass ein **Zustand in der Vergangen-
    heit begonnen** hat und **jetzt noch
    andauert** (oft mit *since* oder *for*).

- Mit dem *present perfect progressive*
drückt man aus, dass ein **Vorgang** oder
eine **Handlung in der Vergangenheit
begonnen** hat und **jetzt noch andauert**.

! Im Deutschen steht oft das Präsens, wo im
Englischen *present perfect* oder *present
perfect progressive* stehen muss.

12.3 **Past perfect, past perfect progressive**

Past perfect

When Robert got to the party, the other guests
had already arrived.

▶ *Past perfect: 17*

- Mit dem *past perfect* drückt man aus,
dass etwas **noch vor etwas anderem** in
der Vergangenheit stattgefunden hatte.

Additional information

Past perfect progressive

At 12 o'clock, Ashley's guests were pretty tired.
They **had been dancing** for hours.

▶ *Past perfect progressive: 18*

- Mit dem *past perfect progressive* wird ausgedrückt, dass eine Handlung vor einem
Zeitpunkt in der Vergangenheit begonnen
hatte und bis (oder fast bis) zu jenem Zeitpunkt andauerte.

Sieh dir die Bilder gut an und vervollständige die Sätze.

a) Simple past *oder* **past progressive**?

When the earthquake started, ...
1 ... Mrs Brown (**make**) tea.
2 ... Mrs Brown (**run**) out of the house.

When the lion escaped, ...
3 ... John Webster (**have**) a sandwich.
4 ... John Webster (**have**) a heart attack.

b) Simple past *oder* **past perfect**?

Helen didn't go to the cinema because ...
1 ... she (**leave**) her purse at home.
2 ... the queue (**be**) too long.

Jacob bought lots of apples because ...
3 ... they (**be**) very cheap.
4 ... his mum (**ask**) him to get some fruit.

c) Simple past *oder* **present perfect**?

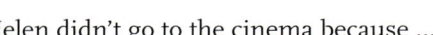

1 *Noah:* Another hour, then we'll take a break.
   Luke: But we (already – **cycle**) 20 km!
   Noah: Come on. Yesterday we (**cycle**) 50 km
         without stopping.

2 *Grace:* What about 'Island Dreams'?
   Kylie: But we (**see**) it! We (**go**) to see it last
          Friday. At the Odeon, remember?

13 **The simple past**
(Die einfache Form der Vergangenheit)   3 : 1 / 3 : 4

13.1 **Form (Form)**

I/You **played**	I/You **didn't play**	**Did** I/you **play?**
He/She/It **played**	He/She/It **didn't play**	**Did** he/she/it **play?**
We/You/They **played**	We/You/They **didn't play**	**Did** we/you/they **play?**

▶ *Kurzformen: 62*

! (to) phone, (to) dance, ... + **-ed** → phoned, danced, ...
(to) plan, (to) stop, ... + **-ed** → pla**nn**ed, sto**pp**ed, ...
(to) try, (to) copy, ... + **-ed** → tr**i**ed, cop**i**ed, ...

▶ *Unregelmäßige Verben: 63*

- Bei **regelmäßigen Verben** bildet man das *simple past* durch Anhängen von **-ed** an den Infinitiv.

- **Unregelmäßige Verben** haben eigene *simple past*-Formen, z. B. *(to) go – **went**, (to) say – **said**, (to) write – **wrote**.*

- **Verneinte Sätze** bildet man mit **didn't**, **Fragen** mit **did**. (Das Vollverb steht im Infinitiv.)

13.2 **Use (Gebrauch)**

When did you move to Freiburg?
– Well, we left Kiel **in 2002** and moved to Potsdam first, and **in 2003** I was offered a job in Freiburg.

Das *simple past* wird verwendet,

- um auszudrücken, dass etwas **zu einem bestimmten Zeitpunkt** oder **in einem bestimmten abgeschlossenen Zeitraum** in der **Vergangenheit** geschah.
Oft stehen Zeitangaben wie *yesterday, three weeks ago, last year, in 2002, on April 4th, ...* in *simple past*-Sätzen.

- wenn man über **vergangene Ereignisse** berichtet oder **eine Geschichte erzählt**.

Woman hurt in traffic accident

A woman was hurt in a traffic accident at the corner of Elm Street and Park Road yesterday morning. A young man on a bike ran into her so that she fell and broke her leg. The man did not stop to help, he just cycled on. Two schoolchildren called an ambulance, and the woman was taken to hospital.

K Last week I lost my watch,
and yesterday someone stole my mobile.
(*not:* Last week I have lost ...,
    and yesterday someone has stolen ...)
Letzte Woche habe ich meine Uhr verloren,
und gestern hat mir jemand das Handy gestohlen.

When did you phone?   (*not:* When have you phoned?)
Wann hast du angerufen?

! Im Deutschen benutzen wir oft das Perfekt, um zu sagen oder zu fragen, **wann** etwas geschah.
Im Englischen muss das *simple past* stehen!

 In *When ...?*-Fragen *simple past*!

▶ *Present perfect oder simple past?: 15.3*

14   **The past progressive**
(Die Verlaufsform der Vergangenheit)   3:4

14.1   **Form (Form)**

I	was	playing	I	wasn't	playing	Was	I		playing?
You	were	playing	You	weren't	playing	Were	you		playing?
He/She/It	was	playing	He/She/It	wasn't	playing	Was	he/she/it	playing?
We	were	playing	We	weren't	playing	Were	we		playing?
You	were	playing	You	weren't	playing	Were	you		playing?
They	were	playing	They	weren't	playing	Were	they		playing?

▶ *Kurzformen: 62*

Das *past progressive* wird mit **was/were** + **-ing form** gebildet.

14.2   **Use (Gebrauch)**

Police officer   Mr Clarke, what were you doing between 8 and 10 o'clock yesterday morning?

Mr Clarke   I was working in the garden.

Das *past progressive* wird verwendet,

- um auszudrücken, dass zu einer **bestimmten Zeit in der Vergangenheit** eine Handlung oder ein Vorgang gerade **im Gange** und **noch nicht abgeschlossen** war.

- um zu sagen, was **gerade vor sich ging**, als etwas anderes passierte.

The kids in room 10 were having a good time   when suddenly Mrs Walter **came** in.

↑   ↑

past progressive   **simple past**

The sun was shining, birds were singing, dogs were running around. People were sitting on the grass, children were playing and laughing. Suddenly there was a loud noise and everything **changed** …

Man findet das *past progressive* oft in Berichten und Erzählungen:
Es beschreibt dann die Situation oder die „Szene", in der etwas geschah.

!   1   Jason was laying the table when Emma came home.
         Jason war dabei, den Tisch zu decken, …

    2   Jason laid the table when Emma came home.
         Jason deckte den Tisch, …

▶ *Verben, die nicht in der progressive form verwendet werden: 11.2*

! Beachte die Bedeutungsunterschiede:
– In **Satz 1** *(past progressive)* war Jason bereits dabei, den Tisch zu decken, als Emma heimkam.
– In **Satz 2** *(simple past)* begann Jason erst mit dem Tischdecken, als sie heimkam.

15 The present perfect   3:1 / 3:4

15.1 Form (Form)

I've/You've **played**	I/You **haven't played**	**Have** I/you **played?**
He's/She's/It's **played**	He/She/It **hasn't played**	**Has** he/she/it **played?**
We've/You've/They've **played**	We/You/They **haven't played**	**Have** we/you/they **played?**

▶ *Kurzformen: 62*

> **!** (to) phone, (to) dance, ... + **-ed** → phoned, danced, ...
> (to) plan, (to) stop, ... + **-ed** → planned, stopped, ...
> (to) try, (to) copy, ... + **-ed** → tried, copied, ...

▶ *Unregelmäßige Verben: 63*

Das *present perfect* wird mit **have/has** + **Partizip Perfekt** *(past participle)* gebildet.

- Bei **regelmäßigen Verben** bildet man das *past participle* durch Anhängen von **-ed** an den Infinitiv.

- **Unregelmäßige Verben** haben eigene *past participle*-Formen, z. B. *(to) be – **been**, (to) say – **said**, (to) write – **written**.*

15.2 Use (Gebrauch)

Connor has phoned. He's had an accident.
Where's Olivia? – She hasn't arrived **yet**.
Have you **ever** tried Greek food? – Yes, I have.

> Look, Mum, I've cooked lunch for you!

How long have you been a member of the tennis club?
– Since March. / For eight months.
Wie lange bist du (schon) Mitglied des Tennisklubs?
– Seit März. / Seit acht Monaten.

▶ *since und for: 15.4 / Present perfect oder present perfect progressive?: 16.3*

Das *present perfect* wird verwendet,

- um zu sagen, **dass jemand etwas getan hat** oder **dass etwas geschehen ist**. Der Zeitpunkt wird nicht genannt, weil er unwichtig oder unbekannt ist. Oft hat die Handlung **Auswirkungen** auf die Gegenwart oder Zukunft. In *present perfect*-Sätzen stehen häufig unbestimmte Zeitangaben wie *already, always, before, ever, just, never, often, yet*.

- um auszudrücken, dass **ein Zustand in der Vergangenheit begonnen hat** und jetzt noch **andauert**. Im Deutschen benutzt man dafür meist das Präsens.

15.3 Present perfect or simple past?

Present perfect	Simple past
1 Where's Julie? Has she moved?	
2 Yes, she has.	3 She moved to New York in the summer.

Present perfect	Simple past
4 **How long** have you been married to Alex? – **Since** 1997.	5 **When** did you marry Alex? – **In** 1997.

(1) Sprecher A fragt, **ob** (nicht: wann) Julie fortgezogen ist → ***present perfect***.
(2) Sprecher B bestätigt, **dass** sie fortgezogen ist → ***present perfect***.
(3) Dann fügt Sprecher B hinzu, **wann** der Umzug erfolgte → ***simple past***.

(4) **How long?** („Seit wann?"/„Wie lange?") → ***present perfect***.
(5) **When?** („Wann?") → ***simple past***.

15.4   *since* and *for* („seit")

It's **five o'clock**. The children are playing football.

They**'ve been** in the park since two o'clock.
... seit zwei Uhr

They**'ve been** in the park for three hours.
... seit drei Stunden

Deutsch „seit" – Englisch < *since* (Zeit<u>punkt</u>)
for (Zeit<u>raum</u>)

Wenn man sagen will, **seit wann** oder **wie lange** ein Zustand bereits andauert, verwendet man das *present perfect* mit *since* bzw. *for*:

- Mit *since* gibt man einen **Zeit**punkt an (*since 2 o'clock; since 2004; since May*). *since* + **Zeit**punkt drückt also aus, **seit wann** ein Zustand andauert.

- Mit *for* gibt man einen **Zeit**raum an (*for three hours; for years; for a long time*). *for* + **Zeit**raum drückt also aus, **wie lange** ein Zustand bereits andauert.

K   We've lived in this flat for 14 years.
Wir wohnen seit 14 Jahren in dieser Wohnung.
(*not:* We live in this flat for 14 years.)

I've had a dog since 2006.
Ich habe einen Hund seit 2006.
(*not:* I have a dog since 2006.)

!   Im Deutschen benutzen wir meist das **Präsens**:   *Wir* **wohnen** *... seit ...*
I **habe** *... seit ...*

Im Englischen muss das **present perfect** stehen: *We***'ve lived** *... for ...*
*I***'ve had** *... since ...*

▶ *Present perfect oder present perfect progressive?: 16.3*

16   **The present perfect progressive**
(Die Verlaufsform des *present perfect*)   3:1 / 3:4

16.1   **Form (Form)**

I've **been playing**	I **haven't been playing**	**Have** I **been playing?**
You've **been playing**	You **haven't been playing**	**Have** you **been playing?**
He's/She's/It's **been playing**	He/She/It **hasn't** **been playing**	**Has** he/she/it **been playing?**
We've **been playing**	We **haven't been playing**	**Have** we **been playing?**
You've **been playing**	You **haven't been playing**	**Have** you **been playing?**
They've **been playing**	They **haven't been playing**	**Have** they **been playing?**

▶ *Kurzformen: 62*

Das *present perfect progressive* wird mit **have/has been** + **-ing form** gebildet.

16.2   Use (Gebrauch)

Little Stevie is in the park, too.

He**'s been watching** them   since two o'clock.
for three hours.

Er sieht ihnen (schon) seit zwei Uhr/seit drei Stunden zu.

▶ *since und for: 15.4*

Mit dem ***present perfect progressive*** drückt man aus, dass eine **Handlung** oder ein **Vorgang** in der Vergangenheit begonnen hat und bis jetzt **andauert**.

K   You**'ve been driving** all night. Shall I drive now?
Du fährst jetzt schon die ganze Nacht. ...
(*not:* You're driving all night.)

I**'ve been trying** to reach her for hours.
Ich versuche seit Stunden, sie zu erreichen.
(*not:* I'm trying to reach her for hours.)

!   Im Deutschen benutzen wir meist das **Präsens**: *Du **fährst** schon die ganze Nacht.*
 *Ich **versuche** seit Stunden ...*

Im Englischen muss das ***present perfect progressive*** stehen:
 *You**'ve been driving** all night.*
 *I**'ve been trying** ... for hours.*

16.3   Present perfect or present perfect progressive?

Present perfect progressive

Ella **has been writing** letters all morning.
Ella schreibt schon den ganzen Morgen Briefe.

Present perfect

Ella **has written** three letters since breakfast.
Ella hat seit dem Frühstück drei Briefe geschrieben.

● Wenn es darum geht, dass eine Tätigkeit **noch andauert**
 → ***present perfect progressive***

● Wenn es darum geht, dass etwas **geschehen ist** (es liegt ein **Ergebnis** vor; es gibt **Auswirkungen** auf Gegenwart oder Zukunft) → ***present perfect***

!   We**'ve been** here all day. Can't we go home now?
Wir sind jetzt (schon) den ganzen Tag hier. ...
I**'ve known** him since kindergarten.
Ich kenne ihn seit dem Kindergarten.
He**'s had** that cold for weeks now, hasn't he?
Er hat diese Erkältung jetzt schon seit Wochen, nicht?

▶ *Verben, die nicht in der progressive form verwendet werden: 11.2*

!   Vorsicht bei Verben, die **Zustände** beschreiben (*be, have, know, like, ...*):
Solche Verben stehen <u>nicht</u> in der Verlaufsform – du musst die einfache Form des *present perfect* verwenden, auch wenn es um das Andauern des Zustands geht.

17   The past perfect (Das Plusquamperfekt)   3:4

17.1   Form (Form)

I/You **had played**	I/You **hadn't played**	Had I/you	**played?**
He/She/It **had played**	He/She/It **hadn't played**	Had he/she/it	**played?**
We/You/They **had played**	We/You/They **hadn't played**	Had we/you/they	**played?**

▶ *Kurzformen: 62*

Das *past perfect* wird mit **had** + **Partizip Perfekt** *(past participle)* gebildet.

▶ *Bildung des Partizip Perfekt: 15.1*

K   I **had** never **tried** Indian food before. It tasted great!
Ich hatte noch nie indisches Essen **probiert**. ...

! Das deutsche Plusquamperfekt wird – je nach Verb – mit „hatte" oder mit „war" gebildet, das *past perfect* immer mit *had*.

Kate's train **had** already **left** when she got to the station.
Kates Zug war schon **abgefahren**, als sie am Bahnhof ankam.

Deutsch „hatte" oder „war" – Englisch *had*

17.2   Use (Gebrauch)

1 Grace **had** already **left** the restaurant when I arrived.
Grace hatte das Restaurant schon verlassen, als ich eintraf.

2 I couldn't open the door. I **had forgotten** the keys.
Ich konnte die Tür nicht öffnen. Ich hatte die Schlüssel vergessen.

3 Grandpa **had** already **been** in hospital for a week when we returned from Spain.
Opa lag schon eine Woche im Krankenhaus, als wir aus Spanien zurückkehrten.

Mit dem ***past perfect*** (Plusquamperfekt oder <u>Vor</u>vergangenheit) drückt man aus,

– dass eine Handlung noch **vor** einer anderen Handlung in der Vergangenheit stattgefunden hatte (1, 2)

– dass ein Zustand noch **vor** einem Zeitpunkt in der Vergangenheit begonnen hatte (3).

!   1 Jason **had laid** the table when Emma came home.
Jason hatte den Tisch (bereits) gedeckt, als Emma heimkam.

2 Jason **laid** the table when Emma came home.
Jason deckte den Tisch, als Emma heimkam.

! Beachte die Bedeutungsunterschiede:
– In **Satz 1** *(past perfect)* war Jason mit dem Tischdecken fertig, als Emma heimkam.

– In **Satz 2** *(simple past)* begann Jason erst mit dem Tischdecken, als sie heimkam.

After she **had left** school she went to university.
oder After she **left** school she went to university.

Nach *after* („nachdem") steht oft *simple past* statt *past perfect*, weil die Reihenfolge der Ereignisse klar ist.

┌─ **Additional information** ───

18 **The past perfect progressive**
     (Die Verlaufsform des *past perfect*)   4:5

18.1 **Form (Form)**

I/You **had been playing**	I/You **hadn't been playing**	Had I/you **been playing?**
He/She/It **had been playing**	He/She/It **hadn't been playing**	Had he/she/it **been playing?**
We **had been playing**	We **hadn't been playing**	Had we **been playing?**
You **had been playing**	You **hadn't been playing**	Had you **been playing?**
They **had been playing**	They **hadn't been playing**	Had they **been playing?**

▶ *Kurzformen: 62*

Das *past perfect progressive* wird mit
had been + ***-ing form*** gebildet.

18.2 **Use (Gebrauch)**

It was nearly six o'clock, and we were tired and hungry.
We **had been working** in the garden all afternoon.
... Wir hatten den ganzen Nachmittag im Garten gearbeitet.

Jaden **had been sitting** in the kitchen for half an hour when
his mum came down.
Jaden hatte eine halbe Stunde lang in der Küche gesessen, ...

Mit dem *past perfect progressive* drückt man
aus, dass eine Handlung oder ein Vorgang vor
einem Zeitpunkt in der Vergangenheit begonnen
hatte und bis zu diesem Zeitpunkt andauerte.

└──

19 **The future – in a nutshell**
     (Die Zukunft – das Wichtigste in Kürze)   3:2 / 3:5

will-future

Jo will be back at six. Can you phone again then?
My mother will be 40 next year.
I expect it will be very hot in Portugal, but I'm
sure you'll like it.

▶ *will-future: 20*

going to-future

I'm going to study history at university.

Look at those clouds. It's going to rain.

▶ *going to-future: 21*

Simple present / Present progressive

The next train to London leaves at 8.45.
The meeting starts in 20 minutes.

We're having a party on Friday. Even our friends
from Glasgow are coming.

▶ *Simple present mit futurischer Bedeutung: 10.2*
▶ *Present progressive mit futurischer Bedeutung: 11.2*

■ Mit dem *will-future* äußert man
Vorhersagen über die Zukunft und
Vermutungen. Oft geht es dabei um
Dinge, die man nicht beeinflussen kann
(z.B. das Alter, das Wetter).

■ Das *going to-future* verwendet man,
 – um über **Absichten, Vorhaben, Pläne**
   für die Zukunft zu sprechen.
 – um auszudrücken, dass etwas **wahrscheinlich gleich passieren** wird
   (es gibt schon deutliche Anzeichen).

■ Auch *simple present* (timetable future)
und *present progressive* (diary future)
können sich auf die Zukunft beziehen.

Vervollständige die Sätze mit der passenden Futurform.

1 Grandma ... 80 next week.   (will be / is going to be)
   We ... a big party for her.   ('ll have / 're going to have)

2 Have you got any plans for this summer?
   – Yes, we ... to California.   ('ll fly / 're going to fly)

3 Do you like your new flat? – Well, it's too
   small, really. We ... out again. We've already   ('ll move / 're going to move)
   started looking.

4 Are you free next Friday? – No, I ... Joanna.   ('m meeting / 'll meet)

5 Don't forget to take some warm clothes.
   It ... cold in Canada at this time of the year. ('ll be / 's going to be)

---

20   **The *will*-future (Das Futur mit *will*)**   3 : 2

20.1   **Form (Form)**

I/You **will play**	I/You **won't play**	**Will** I/you	**play?**
He/She/It **will play**	He/She/It **won't play**	**Will** he/she/it	**play?**
We/You/They **will play**	We/You/They **won't play**	**Will** we/you/they	**play?**

▶ *Kurzformen: 62*

Das *will-future* wird mit **will** + **Infinitiv** gebildet.
Die verneinte Form heißt **won't** (= **will not**).

20.2   **Use (Gebrauch)**

I suppose it will be quite hot in Florida in March.

It's possible you'll find her a bit rude at first, but I think you'll like her.

Das **will-future** wird verwendet,

There will be strong winds tomorrow morning, and we will have some rain in the early afternoon. Temperatures will reach 22 degrees Celsius.

■ um **Vermutungen** und **Vorhersagen** über die Zukunft zu äußern.
In **Vermutungen** stehen oft Ausdrücke wie *I think, I'm sure, I suppose, maybe, probably.*
Bei **Vorhersagen** geht es oft um Dinge, die man nicht beeinflussen kann, z.B. das Wetter.

This exercise is too difficult for me.
– Oh come on, you can do it. I'll help you.

OK, I promise I'll be back by 10.

Tea or coffee? – I think I'll have tea, please.

■ wenn man sich **spontan** – also ohne es im Voraus geplant zu haben – **zu etwas entschließt**. Oft geht es dabei um **Hilfs-angebote** oder **Versprechen**.
(Im Deutschen steht in diesen Fällen meist das Präsens.)

21 The *going to*-future (Das Futur mit *going to*)   3 : 2

21.1 Form (Form)

I'm **going to play**	I'm not **going to play**	**Am** I **going to play?**
You're **going to play**	You **aren't going to play**	**Are** you **going to play?**
He's/She's/It's **going to play**	He/She/It **isn't going to play**	**Is** he/she/it **going to play?**
We're **going to play**	We **aren't going to play**	**Are** we **going to play?**
You're **going to play**	You **aren't going to play**	**Are** you **going to play?**
They're **going to play**	They **aren't going to play**	**Are** they **going to play?**

▶ *Kurzformen: 62*

Das *going to-future* wird mit
am/are/is + ***going to*** + **Infinitiv** gebildet.

21.2 Use (Gebrauch)

What **are** you **going to do** in Paris?
I**'m going to be** a firefighter when I grow up.

Timo's books
are going to fall.

Das **going to-future** wird verwendet,

- um über **Absichten, Vorhaben, Pläne** für die Zukunft zu sprechen.

- um auszudrücken, dass etwas **wahrscheinlich gleich passieren** wird – es gibt bereits deutliche Anzeichen dafür (im Beispiel links wackelt der Bücherstapel schon bedenklich).

22 The future perfect   3 : 5

22.1 Form (Form)

I/You **will have played**	I/You **won't have played**	**Will** I/you **have played?**
He/She/It **will have played**	He/She/It **won't have played**	**Will** he/she/it **have played?**
We **will have played**	We **won't have played**	**Will** we **have played?**
You **will have played**	You **won't have played**	**Will** you **have played?**
They **will have played**	They **won't have played**	**Will** they **have played?**

▶ *Kurzformen: 62*

Das *future perfect* wird mit **will have** +
Partizip Perfekt *(past participle)* gebildet.

▶ *Bildung des Partizip Perfekt: 15.1*

22.2 Use (Gebrauch)

Hurry up, or the last train **will have left** when we get to the station.
Beeil dich, oder der letzte Zug wird abgefahren sein, …

Next June we **will have lived** here ten years.
Nächsten Juni werden wir zehn Jahre hier gewohnt haben.

Mit dem **future perfect** drückt man aus, dass etwas zu einem bestimmten Zeitpunkt in der Zukunft **geschehen oder getan sein wird**. (Im Deutschen nennt man diese Zeit „vollendete Zukunft" oder „Futur II".)

23 Modal auxiliaries (Modale Hilfsverben)   3:5

23.1 Form and characteristics (Form und Eigenschaften)

can	might	needn't	will
could	must	shall	would
may	mustn't	should	

► *Kurzformen: 62*

May we **go** to the disco tonight?
– Yes, you **may**. / No, you **may not**.

I/You/He/She/It/We/You/They **can speak** English.

1 **Can** I help you with those bags?
2 **Can** I go to Ashley's party on Friday?

3 I'd love **to be able to** speak Spanish.
   Ich würde liebend gern Spanisch sprechen können.
4 I hate **having to** get up early.
   Ich hasse es, früh aufstehen zu müssen.
5 We **weren't allowed to** use a dictionary in the test.
   Wir durften beim Test kein Wörterbuch benutzen.

► *can, may, must und ihre Ersatzverben: 23.5–23.7*

23.2 Use (Gebrauch)

You **can** take the car. I **can** go by bike.
Don't you think we **should** ask Mr Carter first?
I **must** go shopping. The fridge is nearly empty.

There's somebody at the door.
– It **may** be the postman.   Es ist vielleicht der Briefträger.
– It **could** be the postman.   Es könnte ... sein.
– It **must** be the postman.   Es muss ... sein.
– It **will** be the postman.   Es wird ... sein.
No, it **can't** be the postman.   Es kann nicht ... sein.

- Modale Hilfsverben (englisch: *modal auxiliaries* oder *modals*) werden zusammen **mit dem Infinitiv eines Vollverbs** verwendet. (Nur in Kurzantworten können sie allein stehen.)

- Verneinung und Frage werden **ohne *do/does/did*** gebildet.

- Modale Hilfsverben haben nur **eine Form**. Es gibt keine Endungen auf *-s*, *-ing* oder *-ed*.

- Modale Hilfsverben beziehen sich in der Regel auf die **Gegenwart** (1) oder auf die **Zukunft** (2).

- Modale Hilfsverben können **nicht alle Zeitformen** bilden. Daher gibt es zu bestimmten modalen Hilfsverben **Ersatzverben** mit ähnlicher Bedeutung, von denen man den Infinitiv (3), die *-ing*-Form (4) und alle Zeitformen (5, *simple past*) bilden kann.

- Modale Hilfsverben drücken aus, dass jemand etwas tun **kann, darf, soll, muss, ...**

- Sie können auch ausdrücken, für wie **sicher, wahrscheinlich** oder **möglich** der Sprecher etwas hält.

That will be the postman.

No, it can't be the postman. It's too early.

23.3 **Overview: What do modal auxiliaries express?**
(Übersicht: Was drücken modale Hilfsverben aus?)

can

Fähigkeit	My grandfather can walk on his hands.
Erlaubnis/Verbot	You can take the car if you like. / You can't smoke in here.
Bitte/Aufforderung	Can I borrow your ruler? / Can you open the window, please?
Möglichkeit	It can't be the postman. It's too early.

could

Fähigkeit (Vergangenheit)	I could swim when I was four.	konnte
Erlaubnis (Vergangenheit)/	I could stay up till ten o'clock when I was 14.	konnte, durfte
Verbot (Vergangenheit)	We couldn't leave the hostel. We had to stay in after 11.	konnten, durften
Bitte/Aufforderung	Could you help me with this exercise?	könntest
Möglichkeit	The phone? At this time of night? Who could that be?	könnte

may

Erlaubnis/Verbot	May I leave a bit earlier today? / This room may not be used by students.
Angebot	May I help you?
Möglichkeit	He may still be at school.

might

| Möglichkeit | There might be some rain later in the afternoon. |

must

| Zwang, Notwendigkeit | You're ill. You must stay in bed. |
| Wahrscheinlichkeit | That boy over there must be Jessica's brother. |

mustn't

| Verbot | You mustn't feed the animals. If you do, they'll get ill. | **!** darfst nicht |

needn't

| Fehlen eines Zwangs/ einer Notwendigkeit | You needn't feed the animals. I've fed them. | **!** brauchst nicht, musst nicht |

shall

| Vorschlag | Shall we take the bus? Or shall I phone for a taxi? |

should

Ratschlag	I think you should go and see a doctor.
Verpflichtung	Hats and coats should be left at the door.
Wahrscheinlichkeit	They should be home by now.

will ▸ *will-future: 20*

| Vorhersage, Vermutung | I'm sure it will be very hot in Greece in August. |
| Wahrscheinlichkeit | Ah, the phone! That will be Uncle Henry. |

would ▸ *would im Bedingungssatz: 48–49*

| Bitte/Aufforderung | Would you pass the sugar, please? |
| Angebot | Would you like some more coffee? |

23.4 *needn't or mustn't?*

Let's order a pizza, then we **needn't** leave the house.

You're ill. You **mustn't** leave the house.

> ■ **keine Notwendigkeit:** *needn't*
>
> *You needn't help me.*
> Du <u>musst</u> mir nicht helfen. /
> Du <u>brauchst</u> mir nicht zu helfen.

> ■ **Verbot:** *mustn't*
>
> *You mustn't help me.*
> Du <u>darfst</u> mir nicht helfen.

23.5 „können": *can – (to) be able to*

Most kids can use a computer. /
Most kids are able to use a computer.

My sister was able to ride a bike when she was four. /
My sister could ride a bike when she was four.

Could you read when you were five? I couldn't.

I could hear music, but I couldn't see anybody.

Have you been able to contact the phone company?
Hast du die Telefonfirma erreichen können?

Jo is ill. He won't be able to come tomorrow.
Jo ist krank. Er wird morgen nicht kommen können.

■ *present tense:*
can und *am/is/are able to*

■ *past tense:*
was/were able to und *could*
could steht vor allem in verneinten Sätzen und Fragen und mit Verben der Wahrnehmung *(see, hear, feel, …)*.

■ *present perfect:*
have/has been able to

■ *will-future:*
will be able to

23.6 „dürfen": *can, may – (to) be allowed to*

Can/May I go to Ashley's party on Friday, Mum?
Are you allowed to go to Ashley's party?

Yesterday we were allowed to watch the late film on TV.
On Saturdays we could always stay up till midnight.

I've always been allowed to wear what I like.
Ich habe schon immer anziehen dürfen, was ich will

I don't know if I'll be allowed to go to the disco on Friday.
Ich weiß nicht, ob ich am Freitag in die Disko gehen darf.

Jeans must not be worn at this school.
Jeans dürfen an dieser Schule nicht getragen werden.
At some schools you're not allowed to wear jeans.
An manchen Schulen darf man keine Jeans tragen.

■ *present tense:*
can, *may* und *am/is/are allowed to*

■ *past tense:*
was/were allowed to und *could*

■ *present perfect:*
have/has been allowed to

■ *will-future:*
will be allowed to

! Für ausdrückliche Verbote wird *mustn't* oder *be not allowed to* verwendet.

23.7 „müssen": *must – (to) have to*

Jo can go to the party, but he has to be back by 11 o'clock.
Jo's mother said: 'You must be back by 11 o'clock.'

You don't have to wear a dress, you can wear jeans. /
You needn't wear a dress, you can wear jeans.
Du musst kein Kleid anziehen, …

I had to get up really early this morning – at 5 o'clock!
When did you have to get up?

We've never had to do so much homework.
Wir haben noch nie so viele Hausaufgaben machen müssen.

You will have to work harder this year.
Du wirst dieses Jahr härter arbeiten müssen.

Do you have to wear a school uniform at your school?
Did you have to tell Hannah that I kissed Sophia?
I felt ill, but I didn't have to see the doctor.

- *present tense:*
  have/has to und *must* (*have to* ist häufiger als *must*, auch in der Gegenwart!)

  Um auszudrücken, dass jemand etwas **nicht tun muss**:
  do/does not have to oder *needn't*

- *past tense:*
  had to

- *present perfect:*
  have/has had to

- *will-future:*
  will have to

! *(to) have to* ist ein Vollverb, also werden Fragen und Verneinungen im *simple present* und *simple past* mit *do/does/did* gebildet.

Did you have to tell Hannah that I kissed Sophia at your party?

a) Vervollständige die Sätze mit passenden Formen von (to) be able to, (to) be allowed to, (to) have to.

1 Our DVD player didn't work any more, so we … buy a new one.
2 Do you think we … use a dictionary in our English test tomorrow? I hope so.
3 There was snow and ice on the road, but the driver … stop the car.
4 Little Jenny fell into the swimming pool. Luckily, she … pull herself out.
5 I'm sorry, I … go in a couple of minutes. I've got an appointment with the head teacher.
6 I (not) … take my pocket knife on my flight to New York last week.

b) mustn't *oder* needn't?

1 You … tell Dad about the trip. He already knows.
2 You … tell Mum about the trip. It's a surprise.

24   The passive (Das Passiv)   3:3 / 4:3

24.1   Active and passive (Aktiv und Passiv)

	Subject			
Active:	William Herschel	discovered	Uranus in 1781.	
	William Herschel	entdeckte Uranus im Jahr 1781.		
Passive:	Uranus	was discovered	in 1781.	
	Uranus	wurde im Jahr 1781 entdeckt.		

Man kann einen Vorgang auf zwei verschiedene Weisen beschreiben:

- Man kann einen **Aktivsatz** verwenden und sagen, **wer oder was etwas tut**. Der Beispielsatz sagt etwas über <u>Herschel</u> aus: *Herschel entdeckte ...*
- Man kann einen **Passivsatz** verwenden und sagen, **mit wem oder womit etwas geschieht**. Der Beispielsatz sagt etwas über <u>Uranus</u> aus: *Uranus wurde ... entdeckt.*

24.2   Form (Form)

Simple present	Lots of cars	are	stolen.
	... werden gestohlen.		
Simple past	Lots of cars	were	stolen.
	... wurden gestohlen.		
Present perfect	Lots of cars	have been	stolen.
	... sind gestohlen worden.		
Past perfect	Lots of cars	had been	stolen.
	... waren gestohlen worden.		
***will*-future**	Lots of cars	will be	stolen.
	... werden gestohlen werden.		
***going to*-future**	Lots of cars	are going to be	stolen.
	... werden gestohlen werden.		
Modal auxiliaries	Lots of cars	could/might be	stolen.
	... könnten gestohlen werden.		

Das Passiv wird mit einer **Form von *be* + Partizip Perfekt** (*past participle*) gebildet.

▶ *Bildung des Partizip Perfekt: 15.1*

24.3   Use (Gebrauch)

A 15-year-old boy <u>was injured</u> in an accident in South Tottenham yesterday afternoon. An ambulance <u>was called</u> and the boy <u>was taken</u> to hospital, where he <u>was treated</u> for shock. The driver of the car that hit him is answering police questions at Tottenham police station and

A girl was hit by a taxi when **she** was cycling along Baker Street. **She** fell and hurt her leg. **She** was taken to hospital where **she** was seen by a doctor.

Mit Passivsätzen kann man Handlungen beschreiben, **ohne zu sagen, wer die Handlung ausführt**.
Das Passiv wird daher oft in Nachrichten, in Zeitungsartikeln, in technischen Beschreibungen und auf Schildern verwendet, wenn man den „Täter" oder „Verursacher" nicht nennen kann oder nicht nennen will.

Oft wechselt man zwischen Aktiv- und Passivsätzen, wenn man mehrere Aussagen über dieselbe Person oder Sache macht.

Coats should be left at the door.
Mäntel sollte man am Eingang abgeben.

Two helicopters could be seen.
Man konnte zwei Hubschrauber sehen.

Im Deutschen werden englische Passivsätze oft durch einen Aktivsatz mit „man"
wiedergegeben.

24.4 Passive sentences with *by* ... (Passivsätze mit *by* ...)

The planet Uranus **was discovered** by **William Herschel**.
... wurde von William Herschel entdeckt.

Half the village **was destroyed** by **an earthquake**.
... wurde durch ein Erdbeben zerstört.

Wenn man in einem Passivsatz den „Täter"
oder „Verursacher" nennen will, verwendet
man die Präposition **by** („von", „durch").

Vervollständige die Passivsätze. Achte auf die richtige Zeitform.

1 Manchester United's stadium (call) 'Old Trafford'. It (build) in 1909.
   *Manchester United's stadium **is called** 'Old Trafford'. It ...*
2 Maps and guide books (can – buy) at the visitor centre.
3 The new motorway (open) by the Queen next Saturday.
4 Hundreds of concert tickets (already – sell).
5 Butter (should – keep) in the fridge.
6 In 1906, more than 2000 people (kill) in an earthquake in California.
7 Fires that broke out after the earthquake (could – not – put out) for days.

24.5 The passive of verbs with two objects (Das Passiv von Verben mit zwei Objekten)

ACTIVE	Indirect object	Direct object	
The company offered	her	a TV role.	
Die Firma bot	ihr	eine Fernsehrolle	an.

Manche Verben können <u>zwei Objekte</u> nach
sich haben:
– ein **indirektes Objekt (Personenobjekt)**
– ein **direktes Objekt (Sachobjekt)**.
Beispiele: *give, offer, pay, send, show, tell*.
▶ *Sätze mit zwei Objekten: 5*

K PASSIVE (English)*

Subject		
She	**was offered**	a TV role.

PASSIVE (German)

Dativobjekt	Subjekt	
Ihr	wurde eine Fernsehrolle	angeboten.

■ Im **Englischen** wird meist das **indirekte
Objekt (Personenobjekt)** zum Subjekt
des Passivsatzes.*
Diese Art des Passivs wird *personal
passive* („persönliches Passiv") genannt.

■ Im **Deutschen** kann nur das **direkte
Objekt (Sachobjekt)** zum Subjekt des
Passivsatzes werden (hier: *eine Fern-
sehrolle*). Die Dativform des Personen-
objekts bleibt im Passivsatz erhalten:
***Ihr** wurde eine Fernsehrolle angeboten.*

* *Manchmal wird auch das **direkte Objekt (Sachobjekt)** zum Subjekt des
Passivsatzes. Das Personenobjekt wird dann meist mit **to** angehängt:*
A TV role was offered **to her.**

Weitere Beispiele für das *personal passive*
findest du auf S. 34.

We **were given** the key and went straight up to our room.
Wir bekamen den Schlüssel und gingen geradewegs auf unser
Zimmer. / Uns wurde der Schlüssel gegeben ...

He **was paid** a lot of money for his book.
Ihm wurde eine Menge Geld gezahlt für sein Buch. /
Er bekam viel Geld für sein Buch.

She **was promised** two million dollars per year.
Ihr wurden zwei Millionen Dollar pro Jahr versprochen. /
Man hat ihr zwei Millionen Dollar pro Jahr versprochen.

Vergleiche die englischen Passivsätze mit
ihren deutschen Übersetzungen.

Additional information

We **were joined** by a group of American tourists.
Eine Gruppe amerikanischer Touristen schloss sich uns an.

They **were thanked** for their work.
Ihnen wurde für ihre Arbeit gedankt. / Man dankte ihnen ...

The earthquake **will be remembered** for a long time.
Man wird sich noch lange an das Erdbeben erinnern.

Das *personal passive* kann auch von Verben
mit <u>einem</u> Objekt wie *help sb., join sb., thank sb.,
remember sth.* gebildet werden.
Vergleiche wieder die englischen Sätze mit
ihren deutschen Übersetzungen.

Wähle ein passendes Verb aus dem Kästchen und vervollständige die Sätze.

1 My grandparents ... a very funny postcard.
   My grandparents **were sent** ...
2 On my first day at school I ... all the classrooms.
3 I was shocked when I ... the news.
4 You **will** ... a few minutes to read the questions before the test begins.
5 You won't believe it! I've ... a job at the local gym.

give • offer • send •
show • tell

25 Question tags (Frageanhängsel)

25.1 Use (Gebrauch)

You've been here before, haven't you?
Du warst schon mal hier, nicht wahr?

You didn't have to pay, did you?
Du musstest nicht bezahlen, ne?

We can start now, can't we?
Wir können jetzt anfangen, nicht?

Frageanhängsel *(haven't you? / did you? / can't we? / ...)* werden oft in Gesprächen benutzt, wenn man vom Gesprächspartner **Zustimmung** zu seiner Aussage erwartet. Deutsche Frageanhängsel sind zum Beispiel „nicht wahr?", „nicht?", „ne?", „ja?". Die Stimme geht am Ende des Satzes wie bei einem Aussagesatz nach unten, obwohl der Satz mit einem Fragezeichen endet.

25.2 Form (Form)

bejaht		verneint
Sophie	can speak French,	can't she?
'Yesterday'	is a song by the Beatles,	isn't it?
Dad	has repaired the bike,	hasn't he?

verneint		bejaht
Pete	can't swim,	can he?
Chips	weren't invented in Britain,	were they?
You	haven't seen Tim,	have you?
John	didn't hurt you,	did he?

Your parents **live** in Bath, don't they?
Mr Connor **looks** good, doesn't he?
You **met** your girlfriend in Greece, didn't you?

Frageanhängsel bestehen aus einem **Hilfsverb** und dem zum Subjekt passenden **Personalpronomen**.

- Wenn der **Aussagesatz bejaht** ist, ist das **Frageanhängsel verneint**.

- Wenn der **Aussagesatz verneint** ist, ist das **Frageanhängsel bejaht**.

! Enthält ein Satz kein Hilfsverb, sondern nur ein Vollverb, dann steht im Frageanhängsel ***don't, doesn't*** oder ***didn't***.

Ordne die Frageanhängsel den Aussagen zu, z.B. 1 D.

1 Look, that's your mum's car, ...
2 You've had your dog a long time, ...
3 The Browns don't live here any more, ...
4 The weather has been awful this week, ...
5 But you saw her last night, ...
6 We don't have to do all these exercises, ...

A haven't you?
B hasn't it?
C do we?
D isn't it?
E didn't you?
F do they?

26 The infinitive (Der Infinitiv) 4:3

26.1 Forms (Formen)

	Active	Passive
Present infinitive	**(to) find** finden	**(to) be found** gefunden werden
Perfect infinitive	**(to) have found** gefunden haben	**(to) have been found** gefunden worden sein

Es gibt vier Infinitiv-Formen.

26.2 The infinitive without *to* (Der Infinitiv ohne *to*)

Julie **can** speak Russian. — Julie kann Russisch sprechen.
You **needn't** help me. — Du brauchst mir nicht zu helfen.
Paul **doesn't** like Madonna. — Paul mag Madonna nicht.
I **didn't** ask her. — Ich habe sie nicht gefragt.

Der Infinitiv ohne *to* steht nach modalen Hilfsverben *(can, could, may, might, …)* und nach *do/does/did*.

▶ *Modale Hilfsverben: 23*

26.3 The *to*-infinitive (Der Infinitiv mit *to*)

Nice to meet you. — Nett, dich kennenzulernen.
I think it's **time** to go. — …, es ist Zeit zu gehen.
But you **promised** to help me! — … mir zu helfen.

▶ *to-Infinitiv oder Gerundium nach bestimmten Verben?: 27.3*

■ Der *to*-Infinitiv kann einem deutschen Infinitiv mit **„zu"** entsprechen.

Dad has gone to the post office to buy some stamps.
Dad ist zur Post gegangen, **um** Briefmarken **zu kaufen.**

She turned on the radio to listen to the news.
Sie schaltete das Radio ein, **um** Nachrichten **zu hören.**

■ Mit dem *to*-Infinitiv kann ein **Zweck**, ein **Ziel**, eine **Absicht** ausgedrückt werden. (deutsch: Infinitiv mit **„um zu"**)

Verb	Object	*to*-infinitive

Andrew **taught** **his sister** to ride a bike.
Andrew brachte seiner Schwester bei, Rad zu fahren.

May we **ask** **you** not to smoke in the restaurant?
Wir möchten Sie bitten, im Restaurant nicht zu rauchen.

■ Nach bestimmten Verben kann ein **Objekt + *to*-Infinitiv** stehen, z.B. *(to)* **allow/ask/help/teach sb. to do** sth. Im Deutschen steht meist ein Infinitiv mit **„zu"**.

K Grandma **expects us** to be home by 10.
Oma erwartet, dass wir um 10 zu Hause sind.

Mrs Black **told us** to meet in the car park.
Mrs Black sagte, dass wir uns auf dem Parkplatz treffen sollten.

She**'d like the whole class** to help with the festival.
Sie möchte, dass die ganze Klasse beim Fest mithilft.

I've always **wanted her** to kiss me.
Ich habe mir schon immer gewünscht, dass sie mich küsst.

! Auch nach den Verben **cause, expect, tell, want, would like, would love** kann ein **Objekt + *to*-Infinitiv** stehen.
Nach den entsprechenden deutschen Verben steht oft ein **Nebensatz mit „dass"**.
Aber auf die englischen Verben darf kein *that*-Satz folgen!
Vergleiche:
  Wir **wollen**, *dass du uns hilfst.*
  We **want** *you to help us.*
Nicht: *We want ~~that you help us~~.*

They wondered whether to stay or to leave.
Sie fragten sich, ob sie bleiben oder gehen sollten.

● Auf *ask, explain, find out, know, show, tell, wonder* folgt oft eine Kombination aus **Fragewort + *to*-Infinitiv**.
Diese Fügungen entsprechen einem Nebensatz mit modalem Hilfsverb. Vergleiche:
  *I didn't know **who to ask**.*
  *I didn't know **who I should/could ask**.*
  („..., wen ich fragen sollte/könnte.")

Auch auf ***whether*** („ob") kann der ***to*-Infinitiv** folgen.

a) Bilde sinnvolle Sätze mit den Verben aus dem Kästchen. (Manchmal gibt es mehr als eine richtige Lösung.)

1 (The teacher said: 'Jaden, clean the board, please.')
  The teacher – Jaden – clean the board.
2 (The policeman said that I had to wait outside.)
  The policeman – me – wait outside.
3 (We all thought she would win the competition.)
  We all – her – win the competition.
4 (Dad thinks we should tidy up our rooms.)
  Dad – us – tidy up our rooms.

> expect • tell •
> want • would like

b) Vervollständige die Sätze. Welches Fragewort passt?

1 Can you tell me ... get to the cathedral?
2 I wasn't sure ... to believe, my brother or my sister.
3 Computer games are OK if you know ... to stop.
4 I was so embarrassed I didn't know ... to say.

> how • what •
> when • who

27 The gerund (Das Gerundium)   4:1

27.1 The *-ing* form as a noun (Die *-ing*-Form als Nomen)

(to) work + **-ing** → **working**
Jenna is **working** in the garden.

▶ *Verlaufsformen: 8.2, 11, 14, 16, 18*

Reading is fun.   (Vergleiche: **Yoga** is fun.)
I love reading.   (Vergleiche: I love **yoga**.)

Reading **animal stories** is fun.
Tiergeschichten zu lesen... / Das Lesen von Tiergeschichten ...

I love reading **in bed at night**.
Ich liebe es, nachts im Bett zu lesen.

Man kann von jedem Vollverb eine ***-ing*-Form** bilden. Sie wird für die Verlaufsformen *(progressive forms)* benötigt.

Die ***-ing*-Form** kann auch **wie ein Nomen** verwendet werden. Sie wird dann als **Gerundium *(gerund)*** bezeichnet.

Das Gerundium kann – wie ein Verb – erweitert werden, z.B. durch ein **Objekt** *(animal stories)* oder eine **Orts- oder Zeit-angabe** *(in bed at night)*.

27.2 The gerund as subject (Das Gerundium als Subjekt)

Subject	
Cycling	is fun.
Cycling in big cities	can be dangerous.

In großen Städten Rad zu fahren kann gefährlich sein. /
Das Radfahren in großen Städten kann gefährlich sein.

Wie jedes Nomen kann das Gerundium (und seine Erweiterung) **Subjekt** eines Satzes sein.
Im Deutschen wird es oft durch einen Infinitiv mit „zu" oder durch ein Nomen wiedergegeben.

27.3 The gerund as object (Das Gerundium als Objekt)

	Object	
Dad **gave up**	smoking	years ago.
My sister **stopped**	eating meat	when she was 15.

Meine Schwester hat aufgehört, **Fleisch zu essen**, als sie 15 war.

Do you **miss** seeing your friends when you're on holiday?
We **kept (on)** walking till we got to a small village.
I need to **practise** writing essays.

Das Gerundium (und seine Erweiterung) kann auch **Objekt** eines Satzes sein.

K I **enjoy** living in Bath.
Ich genieße es, in Bath zu leben. / Ich lebe gern in Bath.

I can't **imagine** living in Bristol.
Ich kann mir nicht vorstellen, in Bristol zu leben.

My brother	**likes** riding	his bike to school.
	likes to ride	
My sister	**prefers** going	by bus.
	prefers to go	

I'd love (= I **would love**) to live in France.
Would you **like** to go out? – No, I'**d prefer** to stay at home.

! Beachte:
■ Nach manchen Verben **muss** ein weiteres Verb als Gerundium stehen.
Zu diesen Verben gehören *enjoy, finish, give up, imagine, keep (on), miss, practise, stop*.
Im Deutschen verwendet man nach den meisten dieser Verben den Infinitiv.
Im Englischen darf **kein Infinitiv** stehen! Also nie:
I enjoy to live ... / *I can't imagine to live* ...

■ Nach *begin, continue, hate, like, love, prefer, start* kann – bei gleicher Bedeutung – ein Gerundium **oder** ein *to*-Infinitiv stehen.

! Aber nach ***would like***, ***would love***, ***would hate***, ***would prefer*** kann **nur** der *to*-Infinitiv stehen.

27.4 The gerund after prepositions (Das Gerundium nach Präpositionen)

They left the shop **without** paying.
..., ohne zu bezahlen.

After all that singing and dancing, we were thirsty.
Nach all dem Singen und Tanzen ... / Nachdem wir so viel gesungen und getanzt hatten ...

Instead of waiting for the bus, we decided to walk home.
Anstatt auf den Bus zu warten ...

Brunel is famous **for** designing Clifton Suspension Bridge.
Brunel ist berühmt dafür, dass er ... entworfen hat.

Nach einer **Präposition** *(after, at, for, in, instead of, of, with, without, ...)* muss ein **Verb als Gerundium** stehen.

Sieh dir die verschiedenen deutschen Entsprechungen an.

Auf der nächsten Seite findest du eine Reihe von nützlichen Wendungen mit **Präposition + Gerundium**.

Adjective + preposition + gerund

Ryan is afraid of **going** in lifts.	Angst vor etwas haben
Mum is very clever at **repairing** things.	gut/geschickt in etwas sein
I'm excited about **flying** to New York.	aufgeregt sein wegen etwas; sich auf etwas freuen
Are you good or bad at **giving** presentations?	gut/schlecht in etwas sein
My sister is interested in **sailing**.	interessiert sein an etwas; sich für etwas interessieren
We're tired of **waiting**.	genug von etwas haben; etwas satt haben

Noun + preposition + gerund

What are the advantages of **living** in the country?	Vorteil *auf dem Land zu leben/des Landlebens*
They had no chance of **catching** the train.	Chance, Gelegenheit *den Zug zu bekommen*
I like the idea of **giving** a party for Grandma.	Vorstellung, Idee *eine Party für Oma zu geben*
What were your reasons for **moving** to Berlin?	Grund *nach Berlin zu ziehen*
There must be another way of **getting** into the building.	Art und Weise, Weg *ins Gebäude zu gelangen*

Verb + preposition + gerund

Everyone is against **going** to war.	gegen etwas sein
We decided against **taking** the bus.	sich gegen etwas entscheiden
Grandma dreams of **meeting** the Queen.	von etwas träumen
Finally we succeeded in **setting** up the tent.	bei/mit etwas Erfolg haben
They've been talking about **closing** that cinema for months.	über etwas sprechen, von etwas reden
Have you thought of **changing** school?	an etwas denken, etwas in Betracht ziehen
He worries about **losing** his job.	sich Sorgen machen wegen/um etwas

We look forward to **hearing** from you.	**!** Das *to* in *look forward to* („sich freuen auf")
Wir freuen uns darauf, von Ihnen zu hören.	ist eine Präposition. Ein folgendes Verb muss daher als Gerundium stehen.

Gerundium oder to-Infinitiv? Vervollständige die Sätze mit den Verben aus dem Kästchen.

1 We're planning ... our holidays in Cornwall. You'll enjoy ... the waves.
2 Mum and Dad have decided against ... abroad this year.
3 I thought we had decided ... to Spain? I've been looking forward to ... on the beach all day.
4 Have you finished ... your essay?

> fly • go •
> lie • revise •
> spend • surf

Additional information

27.5

The gerund with 'its own subject'
(Das Gerundium mit „eigenem Subjekt")

1 Olivia can't **imagine moving** to Italy.
   Olivia kann sich nicht vorstellen, nach Italien zu ziehen.

■ In **Satz 1** bezieht sich *moving* auf *Olivia*.

2 Olivia can't **imagine** her sister **moving** to Italy.
   Olivia kann sich nicht vorstellen, dass <u>ihre Schwester</u> nach Italien zieht.

■ In **Satz 2** hat das Gerundium *moving* ein eigenes Subjekt: *her sister*.

28   Participles (Partizipien)   4:3

28.1   Forms (Formen)

> **Present participle (-ing)**
>
> | (to) stay | → **staying** | (to) try | → **trying** |
> |---|---|---|---|
> | (to) phone | → **phoning** | (to) plan | → **planning** |
>
> ▶ *Verlaufsformen: 8.2, 11, 14, 16, 18 / Das Gerundium: 27*

> **Past participle, regular verbs (-ed)**
>
> | (to) stay | → **stayed** | (to) try | → **tried** |
> |---|---|---|---|
> | (to) phone | → **phoned** | (to) plan | → **planned** |
>
> **Past participle, irregular verbs**   ▶ *Unregelmäßige Verben: 63*
>
> | (to) go | → **gone** | (to) meet | → **met** |
> |---|---|---|---|
> | (to) take | → **taken** | (to) write | → **written** |

▶ *Perfect tenses: 15, 17, 22 / Das Passiv: 24*

Es gibt zwei Arten von Partizipien:

■ Das **Partizip Präsens** *(present participle)* endet auf *-ing*.
Du kennst die *-ing*-Form von den Verlaufsformen und in der Rolle eines Nomens (als Gerundium).

■ Die 3. Form des Verbs nennt man **Partizip Perfekt** *(past participle)*.
Das Partizip Perfekt der <u>regelmäßigen</u> Verben endet auf *-ed*.
<u>Unregelmäßige</u> Verben haben eigene 3. Formen, die man einzeln lernen muss.
Du kennst das Partizip Perfekt von den *perfect tenses* und vom Passiv.

28.2   Participle clauses instead of relative clauses (Partizipialsätze anstelle von Relativsätzen)

> **Participle clause**
>
> 1   The train arriving **on platform** 5 will continue to Bath.
> Der Zug, der auf Gleis 5 einfährt, …
> 2   Tourists visiting **London** shouldn't miss St Paul's.
> Touristen, die London besuchen, …
>
> 3   What's the name of that song sung **by Lily Allen**?
> Wie heißt dieser Song, der von Lily Allen gesungen wurde?
> 4   The number of accidents caused **by cyclists** has fallen.
> Die Zahl der Unfälle, die von Radfahrern verursacht wurden, …

Partizipialsätze können Relativsätzen entsprechen:

■ Das **_present participle_** (Sätze 1, 2) steht für ein <u>Relativpronomen</u> + **Verb im Aktiv**:
*the train **arriving** on platform 5 =*
*the train **that is arriving** on platform 5*

■ Das **_past participle_** (Sätze 3, 4) steht für ein <u>Relativpronomen</u> + **Verb im Passiv**:
*a song **sung** by Lily Allen =*
*a song **that was sung** by Lily Allen*

Partizip Präsens oder Partizip Perfekt – was ist korrekt?

1   (producing / produced)   Why is wine from Australia often cheaper than wine … in Europe?
2   (travelling / travelled)   On the train we met some American students … through Europe.
3   (designing / designed)   My brother has got a job with a company … computer games.
4   (designing / designed)   They've published a dictionary specially … for students.
5   (playing / played)   Cricket is a game … in many English-speaking countries.

The noun (Das Nomen)

29 The plural of nouns (Der Plural der Nomen)

	Singular		Plural	
one	cat	two	cats	[-s]
	dog		dogs	[-z]
	tree		trees	[-z]
	bus [-s]		buses	[-ɪz]
	bridge [-dʒ]		bridges	[-ɪz]

	Singular		Plural	
one	story	two	stories	
	monkey		monkeys	
one	half, knife, life, shelf, thief, wife	two	halves, knives, lives, shelves, thieves, wives	
one	hero	two	heroes	
	potato		potatoes	
	tomato		tomatoes	
one	child [tʃaɪld]	two	children [ˈtʃɪldrən]	
	man [mæn]		men [men]	
	woman [ˈwʊmən]		women [ˈwɪmɪn]	
	foot		feet	
	mouse		mice	
	tooth		teeth	
one	deer	two	deer	
	dice		dice	
	series		series	
	sheep		sheep	

Der Plural (die Mehrzahl) eines Nomens wird in der Regel mit **-s** gebildet:

Singular + s = Plural

Nach Zischlauten, z.B. [s], [z], [ʃ], [tʃ], [dʒ], wird **-es** oder **-s** angehängt, je nach Schreibung des Singulars.

! **Beachte:**

- **-y** nach **Konsonant** wird zu **-ies**. (Aber **-y** nach **Vokal** bleibt **-y**.)

- Nomen, die auf **-f** oder **-fe** enden, bilden den Plural meist mit **-ves**.

- Die Nomen **hero, potato** und **tomato** bilden den Plural mit **-es**. (Aber: *discos, kilos, photos, pianos, radios, studios, videos*)

- Einige Nomen haben **unregelmäßige Pluralformen**.

30 Plural nouns (Nomen, die nur im Plural stehen)

K Plural im Englischen – Singular im Deutschen

Those **trousers/tights/swimming trunks** are great. Were they expensive?
Die **Hose/Strumpfhose/Badehose** ist toll. War sie teuer?

I need some new **pyjamas**. These are too small.
Ich brauche einen neuen **Schlafanzug**. Dieser ist zu klein.

These **headphones** sound great. Can we buy them?
Dieser **Kopfhörer** klingt toll. Können wir ihn kaufen?

I bought a new pair of **jeans** yesterday.   eine neue Jeans
Why do you need two pairs of **glasses**?   zwei Brillen

Einige englische Nomen werden – anders als ihre deutschen Entsprechungen – **immer im Plural** gebraucht:

- Sie haben keinen Singular und dürfen nicht mit dem unbestimmten Artikel *a* oder mit den Zahlwörtern *one/two/three* usw. verwendet werden.

- Achte darauf, dass auch die zugehörigen Begleiter, Verben und Pronomen im Plural stehen.

Wenn man eine bestimmte Anzahl Hosen, Brillen usw. nennen möchte, muss man **a pair of …, two pairs of …** verwenden.

K **Clothes** are often expensive in small boutiques.
Kleidung ist / **Kleider** sind oft teuer ...

These **stairs** aren't very safe.
Diese **Treppe** ist / Diese **Treppen** sind nicht sehr sicher.

The **cattle** are hungry. You should feed them.
Das **Vieh** hat Hunger / ist hungrig. Du solltest es füttern.

Where are the **police**? Did you call them?
Wo ist die **Polizei**? Hast du sie *(Singular)* gerufen?

! Zu den Nomen, die keinen Singular haben und immer als Plural verwendet werden, gehören auch **clothes** und **stairs** sowie **cattle** („Vieh, Rinder") und **police**.

31 **Uncountable nouns (Nicht zählbare Nomen)**   4 : 4

Zählbare Nomen (Countable nouns)	
a friend – two friends	an idea – some ideas
a book – lots of books	one year – many years

Nicht zählbare Nomen (Uncountable nouns)		
bread *Brot*	**luck** *Glück*	**plastic** *Plastik*
butter *Butter*	**milk** *Milch*	**sugar** *Zucker*
cheese *Käse*	**money** *Geld*	**time** *Zeit*
coffee *Kaffee*	**music** *Musik*	**traffic** *Verkehr*
jewellery *Schmuck*	**paper** *Papier*	**water** *Wasser*

Two **litres of** milk and a **kilo of** sugar, please.
Would you like a **cup of** coffee or a **glass of** water?
There's a **piece of** plastic in my cornflakes.

Die meisten Nomen sind **zählbar** – sie bezeichnen etwas, das man zählen kann. Zählbare Nomen kommen im Singular und im Plural vor.

Nicht zählbare Nomen bezeichnen etwas, das man nicht zählen kann.
Nicht zählbare Nomen haben <u>keinen Plural</u> und stehen nicht mit *a/an* oder *one/two/three* usw. Auch die zugehörigen Begleiter, Verben und Pronomen stehen im Singular.

Wenn man bestimmte Mengen oder eine bestimmte Anzahl nennen möchte, verwendet man passende Wendungen wie *a kilo of ..., a piece of ..., two packets of ...* .

K Camping **equipment** doesn't have to be expensive!
Camping-Ausrüstungen müssen nicht teuer sein!

I like your new **furniture**. Where did you buy it?
Ich mag deine neuen Möbel. Wo hast du sie gekauft?

Your **hair** looks nice. Who cut it?
Deine Haare sehen gut aus. Wer hat sie geschnitten?

That's too much **homework**. I can't do it all tonight.
Das sind zu viele Hausaufgaben. Ich kann sie nicht alle heute Abend machen.

Where did you get this **information**? It's priceless!
Woher hast du diese Information(en)? Sie ist/sind unbezahlbar!

No **news** is good news.   ... sind gute Nachrichten.
The USA is a very big country.   ... sind ein sehr großes Land.

▶ *Mengenangaben bei zählbaren und nicht zählbaren Nomen: 36.1*

! Die folgenden englischen Nomen sind – anders als ihre deutschen Entsprechungen – **nicht zählbar**. Das zugehörige Verb sowie zugehörige Begleiter und Pronomen stehen **im Singular**.

equipment	*Ausrüstung(en)*
experience	*Erfahrung(en)*
furniture	*Möbel*
hair	*Haar(e)*
homework	*Hausaufgabe(n)*
information	*Information(en)*
research	*Forschung(en).*

Auch **news** und **the Unites States/the USA** werden als Singulare verwendet – trotz des Plural-**s**.

Additional information

uncountable	countable
Your **hair** looks great. deine Haare, deine Frisur	There are some **hairs** on your jacket. ein paar (einzelne) Haare
Glass breaks easily. Glas	We need some more **glasses**. mehr Gläser
Is there any **coffee/tea**? Kaffee/Tee	Two **coffees** and two **teas**, please. zwei Kaffee und zwei Tee
Sugar makes you fat. Zucker	Milk and two **sugars**, please. zwei (Stück) Zucker
I need some **paper** for the printer. Papier	Your **papers**, please. Ihre Papiere, bitte.

Manche Nomen können je nach Bedeutung zählbar oder nicht zählbar sein.
Vergleiche die Beispiele links.

a) Vervollständige die Sätze.

1 The international news ... (is/are) at eight o'clock.
2 The police ... (was/were) waiting round the corner, with an ambulance behind ... (it/them).
3 The black trousers ... (is/are) too tight, but the red jeans ... (looks/look) good on you.
4 I have to wear ... (glasses/a glass) when I'm driving, but I don't need ... (it/them) to read.
5 The new equipment for the camera club ... (has/have) arrived. ... (It was/They were) quite expensive, so please be careful.

b) Sieh dir die Bilder an – all das muss eingekauft werden.
Vervollständige die Einkaufsliste mit den Ausdrücken aus dem Kästchen.

2 bottles • 1 kilo •
2 packets • 1 piece •
1/2 pound

Shopping list
1/2 ... of butter
2 ... coffee
1 ...
...
...

32 *s*-genitive and *of*-phrase (*s*-Genitiv und *of*-Fügung)

Is that **John**'s **car** over there? ... Johns Auto
What was **the woman**'s **name**? ... der Name der Frau

Singular:	's	the girl's room das Zimmer des Mädchens
Plural auf -*(e)s*:	'	the girls' room das Zimmer der Mädchen
Plural nicht auf -*(e)s*:	's	the children's room das Zimmer der Kinder

The doors of his **car** were open.   Die Türen seines Autos ...
What's **the name of the street**?   ... der Name der Straße

- Wenn man sagen will, dass etwas **einer Person gehört** (oder zu einer Person gehört), benutzt man den ***s*-Genitiv.**

- Wenn man sagen will, dass etwas **zu einer Sache gehört**, benutzt man die ***of*-Fügung.**

I felt ill and went **to the doctor**'s.	zum Arzt
My sister is **at the hairdresser**'s (shop).	beim Friseur
Is there a **chemist**'s (shop) near here?	eine Apotheke
We went to a party **at the Devlin**'s (house).	bei den Devlins

! Beachte:
- Der *s*-**Genitiv** steht auch bei bestimmten **Ortsangaben**, z.B. bei Geschäften oder Arztpraxen und bei Häusern und Wohnungen von Bekannten. Die Wörter *shop* oder *house/flat* werden weggelassen, sind aber mitgedacht.

Have you read **today**'s **paper** yet?
... die Zeitung von heute / die heutige Zeitung

(on TV) And now for **tomorrow**'s **weather**: ...
... das Wetter von morgen / das morgige Wetter

Do you know **last week**'s **football results**?
... die Fußballergebnisse von letzter Woche / der letzten Woche

- **Zeitangaben** können als *s*-**Genitiv** vor einem Nomen stehen.

two **kilos** of potatoes	zwei Kilo Kartoffeln
a **pound** of salmon	ein Pfund Lachs
a **metre** of rope	ein Meter Seil
a **piece** of cake	ein Stück Kuchen
three **pairs** of shoes	drei Paar Schuhe
two **bottles** of milk	zwei Flaschen Milch
a **glass** of water	ein Glas Wasser
a **packet** of crisps	eine Packung Chips

- Die *of*-**Fügung** wird bei **Maß-** und **Mengenangaben** *(two kilos of ..., a metre of ...)* und bei **Behältnissen** *(two bottles of ..., a packet of ...)* verwendet.

the **city** of Glasgow	die Stadt Glasgow
the **town** of Milton Keynes	die Stadt Milton Keynes
the **island** of Majorca	die Insel Mallorca

- Die *of*-**Fügung** steht in **Ortsangaben** wie *the city of ..., the island of ...*

33 **The prop word *one/ones* (Das Stützwort *one/ones*)**

K This <u>mobile</u> is better than the one you gave me.
Dieses <u>Handy</u> ist besser als das, das du mir gegeben hast.

These <u>boots</u> look nice. What about the black ones?
– I like the red ones better.
Diese <u>Stiefel</u> sehen gut aus. Wie wäre es mit den schwarzen?
– Ich mag die roten lieber.

Wenn man ein schon genanntes zählbares Nomen nicht wiederholen will, muss man **one** (Singular) bzw. **ones** (Plural) verwenden.

Man nennt *one/ones* „Stützwort", weil im Englischen – anders als im Deutschen – Adjektive und der bestimmte Artikel nicht allein stehen können: Sie brauchen eine „Stütze".

Which one would you like to have?
The little one.

Welchen hättest du gern? – Den kleinen.

Das **Stütz**wort *one/ones*

the black one   *the red one*   *the blue one*

Determiners and pronouns (Begleiter und Pronomen)

- **Begleiter** stehen <u>vor</u> einem Nomen:
  the book – *a* girl – *my* CD – *this* road
  – *some* chips – ...

- **Pronomen** (<u>Für</u>wörter, Stellvertreter)
  stehen <u>anstelle</u> eines Nomens:
  it (the book) – *mine* (my CD) – ...

34 Overview (Übersicht)

Articles (Artikel) ▶ 35	the – a/an
Personal pronouns (Personalpronomen)	I – you – he – she – it – we – you – they me – you – him – her – it – us – you – them
Possessive determiners (Possessivbegleiter)	my – your – his – her – its – our – your – their
Possessive pronouns (Possessivpronomen)	mine – yours – his – hers – ours – yours – theirs
Demonstrative determiners/pronouns (Demonstrativbegleiter/-pronomen)	this – that – these – those
Quantifiers (Mengenangaben) ▶ 36	a lot (of) – much – many – a little – a few – some – any – every – no – ...
Reflexive pronouns (Reflexivpronomen) ▶ 37	myself – yourself – himself – herself – itself – ourselves – yourselves – themselves
Relative pronouns (Relativpronomen) ▶ 52	who – which – that – whose

35 The articles (Die Artikel)

35.1 Form and pronunciation (Form und Aussprache)

Bestimmter Artikel			Unbestimmter Artikel		
[ðə] the	boy	der Junge	a	boy	ein Junge
the	door	die Tür	a	door	eine Tür
the	new car	das neue Auto	a	new car	ein neues Auto
the	CDs	die CDs			
[ði] the	uncle	der Onkel	an	uncle	ein Onkel
the	aunt	die Tante	an	aunt	eine Tante
the	old car	das alte Auto	an	old car	ein altes Auto
the	ideas	die Ideen			

Der **bestimmte Artikel** *(definite article)*
heißt *the*, der **unbestimmte Artikel**
(indefinite article) heißt *a* oder *an*.

- Wenn das Nomen (bzw. das Adjektiv) am
  Anfang mit einem **Konsonanten** gesprochen wird, steht der unbestimmte Artikel *a*, und *the* wird [ðə] ausgesprochen.

- Wenn das Nomen (bzw. das Adjektiv) am
  Anfang mit einem **Vokal** gesprochen
  wird, steht der unbestimmte Artikel *an*,
  und *the* wird [ði] ausgesprochen.

!
the uncle [ði_ˈʌŋkl]   the uniform [ðə ˈjuːnɪfɔːm]
an uncle [ən_ˈʌŋkl]   a   uniform [ə ˈjuːnɪfɔːm]

the hour [ði_ˈaʊə]   the house [ðə ˈhaʊs]
an hour [ən_ˈaʊə]   a   house [ə ˈhaʊs]

! Bei einigen wenigen Wörtern könnte die
Schreibung zu Fehlern führen.
Beachte, dass die **Aussprache** des Wortes
entscheidend ist, nicht die Schreibung!

35.2 **The definite article – special cases**
  (Der bestimmte Artikel – Besonderheiten) 3:1 / 4:4

---

allgemein: ohne *the*

Life in London is expensive.	Das Leben in London ...
Noise is bad for your health.	Lärm ...
Green **tea** is delicious.	Grüner Tee ...
Sand is used to make glass.	Sand ...
Children like ice cream.	Kinder ...
Big **cars** need a lot of petrol.	Große Autos ...

---

näher bestimmt: mit *the*

What do you know about the **life** of Madonna?
... das Leben von Madonna
The **noise** in this room is terrible.
Der Lärm in diesem Zimmer ...
The **tea** we got on the train was horrible.
Der Tee, den wir im Zug bekommen haben, ...
The **sand** on this beach doesn't look very clean.
Der Sand an diesem Strand ...
The **children** in our street are all very nice.
Die Kinder in unserer Straße ...
The **cars** that we looked at were all too expensive.
Die Autos, die wir uns angesehen haben, ...

- **Abstrakte Nomen** (*life, love, noise, ...*),
  Stoffbezeichnungen (*tea, oil, sand, ...*)
  und **Nomen im Plural** (*children, cars, ...*)

  – stehen **ohne bestimmten Artikel**,
    wenn sie <u>ganz allgemein</u> verwendet
    werden (in den Beispielen geht es um
    das Leben in London, um Lärm, um
    grünen Tee usw. im Allgemeinen)

  – stehen **mit bestimmtem Artikel**,
    wenn sie <u>näher bestimmt</u> sind,
    z.B. durch eine *of*-Fügung, eine Orts-
    angabe oder einen Relativsatz (in
    den Beispielen geht es um ein ganz
    bestimmtes Leben, um den Lärm in
    einem bestimmten Zimmer usw.).

Funktion/Zweck: ohne *the*

We go **to church** every Sunday.
... in die Kirche *(zum Gottesdienst)*
He spent two years **in prison**.
... im Gefängnis *(um eine Strafe zu verbüßen)*
I know her **from school**.
... aus der Schule *(vom gemeinsamen Unterricht)*
Dad's ill. He's **in hospital**. (*AE:* in <u>the</u> hospital)
... im Krankenhaus *(zur Behandlung)*

Ort/Bauwerk: mit *the*

There's a concert in the **church** on Friday.
He works in one of the factories behind the **prison**.
Go straight on till you get to the **school**, then turn left.

- **Gebäudebezeichnungen** wie
  church, prison, school

  – stehen **ohne bestimmten Artikel**,
    wenn <u>die Funktion / der Zweck</u> des
    Gebäudes im Vordergrund steht

  – stehen **mit bestimmtem Artikel**, wenn
    es um <u>den Ort / das Bauwerk</u> geht.

I live **in Elm Street / in Brick Lane / near Oxford Circus**.
Let's go for a walk **in Hyde Park**.
Let's look **at Trafalgar Square** too.
They've got a little cabin **near Lake Michigan**.
Have you ever seen **Buckingham Palace / St Paul's
Cathedral / Nelson's Column**?

- **Namen** von **Straßen, Plätzen, Parks,
  Seen, Bergen** stehen – anders als
  im Deutschen – in der Regel **ohne
  bestimmten Artikel**, ebenso die Namen
  vieler **Gebäude**.

35.3 The indefinite article – special cases (Der unbestimmte Artikel – Besonderheiten)

My mother is a **dentist**. I'd like to be a **fashion designer**.
Meine Mutter ist Zahnärztin. Ich möchte Modedesigner werden.
After more than 20 years in Berlin, he became a **German**.
Nach mehr als 20 Jahren in Berlin wurde er Deutscher.

- Anders als im Deutschen stehen **Berufs-** und **Nationalitätsangaben** mit **unbestimmtem Artikel**.

My father works **as an** engineer.	... als Ingenieur
You can use your shoe **as a** hammer.	... als Hammer
You can't get to the lake **without a** car.	... ohne Auto

- Anders als im Deutschen steht der **unbestimmte Artikel** nach *as* („als") und nach *without*.

We sell about 60 mobiles a **week**.
... etwa 60 Handys pro Woche / in der Woche / die Woche.
The speed limit is 30 miles an **hour**.
... 30 Meilen pro Stunde / in der Stunde / die Stunde.
Potatoes were 59p a **kilo**.
... 59 Pence pro Kilo / das Kilo / je Kilo.

- Der **unbestimmte Artikel** steht in der Bedeutung „pro", „je" vor **Zeitangaben** und vor **Maß- und Mengenangaben**.

Sieh dir die Sätze an. Was ist korrekt, **A, B** *oder* **C**?

1 My brother is ... paramedic. He works five nights ... week in our local hospital.
2 Mr Jones travels to ... hospital every evening to visit his wife.
3 I think ... bread tastes best when it's fresh.
4 ... bread we bought at the supermarket was old.
5 I don't usually drink ... coffee in the evenings.
6 ... coffee they sell here is so good that I always have two cups. And it's only 50p ... cup.

A	the
B	a
C	– *(no article)*

36 Quantifiers (Mengenangaben)

I met a lot of / lots of surfers on the beach.
There was some cheese but not much bread.
We haven't got any orange juice.

Begleiter	There's some **chocolate** in the kitchen.
Pronomen	Can I have some?

Wenn man über **unbestimmte Mengen** spricht, benutzt man **Mengenangaben** wie *a lot (of), much, many, some, any, every, ...*

Mengenangaben können als Begleiter vor einem Nomen stehen oder als Pronomen verwendet werden. (Ausnahmen: *every* und *no* stehen nur vor Nomen).

36.1 Quantifiers with countable and uncountable nouns (Mengenangaben bei zählbaren und nicht zählbaren Nomen)   4:4

zählbar	Can I have some apples, please?	ein paar
nicht zählbar	Can I have some milk, please?	etwas

zählbar	How many apples have we got?	wie viele
nicht zählbar	How much milk have we got?	wie viel

▶ *Nicht zählbare Nomen: 31*

- Manche Mengenangaben können **sowohl** bei zählbaren **als auch** bei nicht zählbaren Nomen stehen.

- Andere stehen **nur** bei zählbaren oder **nur** bei nicht zählbaren Nomen.

Sieh dir dazu die **Übersicht** auf S. 48 an.

Countable nouns	Uncountable nouns
I'd like a lot of children. ... viele Kinder	I'd like a lot of money. ... viel Geld
I've got some ideas. ... einige/ein paar Ideen	I've got some time. ... etwas Zeit
There aren't any eggs. ... keine Eier (mehr)	There isn't any butter. ... keine Butter (mehr)
There were no CDs. ... keine CDs	There was no music. ... keine Musik
How many CDs have you got? – Not many. Just a few. Wie viele CDs hast du? – Nicht viele. Nur ein paar.	
	How much time have we got? – Not much. Just a little. Wie viel Zeit haben wir? – Nicht viel. Nur ein bisschen.

- *a lot of/lots of, some, any, no*
  verwendet man sowohl mit dem
  Plural von zählbaren Nomen als
  auch mit nicht zählbaren Nomen.
  ▶ *some/any: 36.2*

- *many* („viel**e**") und *(a) few*
  („wenig**e**", „ein paar") werden nur
  mit dem **Plural von zählbaren
  Nomen** verwendet.

- *much* („viel") und *(a) little*
  („wenig", „ein bisschen") werden
  nur mit **nicht zählbaren Nomen**
  verwendet.

- **Plural von zählbaren Nomen:** - **nicht zählbare Nomen:**
  many / (a) few *much / (a) little*

positive	There was a lot of traffic on the motorway.
negative	We **didn't** have much time.
question	Are there many accidents in your street?

There were already a few (= some) people in the queue,
but I didn't have to wait long.   ... ein paar Leute ...
There were few (= not many) people in the streets
so late at night.   ... (nur) wenige Leute ...

They gave her a little (= some) money and sent her to
the shops.   ... etwas/ein bisschen Geld ...
We had very little (= not much) money when we were
young.   ... sehr wenig Geld ...

! **Beachte:**

- In **bejahten Aussagesätzen** steht meist
  a lot of oder *lots of*.
  In **verneinten Aussagesätzen** und in
  Fragen steht meist *much* bzw. *many*.

- *a few* entspricht dem deutschen
  „ein paar".
  few entspricht dem deutschen
  „wenige", „nicht viele".

- *a little* entspricht dem deutschen
  „etwas", „ein bisschen".
  little entspricht dem deutschen
  „wenig", „nicht viel".

Welche Mengenangabe passt in den Satz?

1 (much/some)   We don't get ... snow where we live.
2 (many/much)   I don't drink ... coffee. Just one cup in the morning.
3 (few/a few)   ... people like his books because they're so difficult to read.
4 (some/a few)   I can give you ... money if you need it.
5 (a few/a little)   There are ... apples left in the bowl.

36.2 ***some/any* and their compounds
(*some/any* und ihre Zusammensetzungen)**

I'll go to the shops and get some **eggs**.
I'm thirsty. – There's some **milk** in the fridge.

- ***some***: vor allem in **bejahten Aussage-sätzen**
  Deutsch: „einige" *(some eggs/stamps/...)*
  oder „etwas" *(some milk/money/...)*

We haven't got any **butter**.   ... keine **Butter** (mehr)
Are there any **apples**? – No, there are**n't** any.
Gibt es (noch) **Äpfel**. – Nein, es sind keine mehr da.

- ***any***: vor allem in **verneinten Aussage-sätzen** und in **Fragen**

Für die Zusammensetzungen mit *some*- und *any*- gelten dieselben Regeln:

- **somebody** (oder **someone**), **something**, **somewhere**: vor allem in **bejahten Aussagesätzen**

I think there's someone in the garden. Can you see anyone?

No, I can't see anything. It's too dark.

- **anybody** (oder **anyone**), **anything**, **anywhere**: vor allem in **verneinten Aussagesätzen** und in **Fragen**

Ich glaube, es ist jemand im Garten. Kannst du (irgend)jemanden sehen? – Nein, ich kann nichts sehen. Es ist zu dunkel.

Would you like something to eat? Some cheese and biscuits perhaps? – No, thank you. But could I have something to drink? Some juice or water, please?

You can buy this drink at any supermarket.
And it's healthier than any other soft drink.
... in jedem (beliebigen) Supermarkt ... gesünder als irgendein anderer Softdrink / als alle anderen Softdrinks

When you get off the bus, you can ask anybody the way to the theatre.
... kannst du jeden (Beliebigen) nach dem Weg fragen /
... fragen, wen du willst
I'm so hungry I could eat anything.
... alles (egal was)

! **Beachte:**

- In Fragen, die eigentlich ein **Angebot** oder eine **Bitte** sind, verwendet man ***some, something*** usw.

- ***any*** wird auch in bejahten Aussagesätzen verwendet und bedeutet dann „jeder (beliebige)", „irgendein".

  Auch die Zusammensetzungen mit *any* können so verwendet werden – siehe die Beispiele links.

36.3 ***every ...* – *each ...***

Every **song** / Each **song** will be played twice.

Every **child** likes ice cream.
Jedes Kind ... *(alle Kinder, Kinder im Allgemeinen)*
Each **child** got an ice cream.
Jedes (einzelne) Kind ... *(aus einer bestimmten Gruppe)*

▶ any („jeder beliebige"): 36.2

every ... bzw. *each ...* werden wie das deutsche „jede(r, s)" verwendet.

every und *each* sind oft austauschbar, der Bedeutungsunterschied ist gering: Bei *each* denkt man nicht so sehr an die Gruppe als Ganzes, sondern an jedes einzelne Mitglied.

37   Reflexive pronouns (Reflexivpronomen)   3 : 5 / 4 : 1

37.1   Forms (Formen)

Singular	-self [-'self]	
I've hurt	myself.	Ich habe **mir** wehgetan / **mich** verletzt.
You've hurt	yourself.	Du hast **dir** wehgetan / **dich** verletzt.
He's hurt	himself.	Er hat **sich** wehgetan / **sich** verletzt.
She's hurt	herself.	Sie hat **sich** wehgetan / **sich** verletzt.
It's hurt	itself.	Es hat **sich** wehgetan / **sich** verletzt.

Plural	-selves [-'selvz]	
We've hurt	ourselves.	Wir haben **uns** wehgetan / **uns** verletzt.
You've hurt	yourselves.	Ihr habt **euch** wehgetan / **euch** verletzt.
They've hurt	themselves.	Sie haben **sich** wehgetan / **sich** verletzt.

Bei den Reflexivpronomen liegt die **Betonung auf der zweiten Silbe**:
my*self* [maɪ'self],
our*selves* [aʊə'selvz] usw.

37.2   Use (Gebrauch)

My mother cut herself with the bread knife.
Meine Mutter hat sich mit dem Brotmesser geschnitten.

Is **he** talking to himself or is he speaking on his mobile?
Redet **er** mit sich selbst …?

We're old enough to look after ourselves.
Wir sind alt genug, um auf uns (selbst) aufzupassen.

| **My brother** hurt him. | … ihn verletzt | *(jn. anders)* |
| **My brother** hurt himself. | … sich verletzt | *(sich selbst)* |

Reflexivpronomen beziehen sich zurück auf das Subjekt des Satzes – sie sind **rückbezüglich** (= reflexiv). Sie bezeichnen dieselbe Person oder Sache wie das Subjekt.

Verwechsle nicht Personal- und Reflexivpronomen.

K   Daniel felt very sad after his grandma had died.
Daniel fühlte sich sehr traurig, …

Do you remember the party at Emily's last summer?
Erinnerst du dich an die Party …

!   Es gibt eine Reihe von Verben, die im Deutschen reflexiv sind, im Englischen jedoch nicht.

(to) **argue**	sich streiten	(to) **move**	sich bewegen
(to) **calm down**	sich beruhigen	(to) **open**	sich öffnen
(to) **change**	sich (ver)ändern;	(to) **relax**	sich entspannen;
	sich umziehen		sich ausruhen
(to) **feel**	sich fühlen; sich anfühlen	(to) **remember** sth.	sich an etwas erinnern;
(to) **get dessed**	sich anziehen		sich etwas merken
(to) **hide**	sich verstecken	(to) **sit down**	sich (hin)setzen
(to) **hurry (up)**	sich beeilen	(to) **turn (around)**	sich umdrehen
(to) **imagine** sth.	sich etwas vorstellen	(to) **watch** sth.	sich etwas ansehen
(to) **listen to** sth.	sich etwas anhören	(to) **wonder**	sich fragen
(to) **look forward to**	sich freuen auf	(to) **worry**	sich Sorgen machen
(to) **meet**	sich treffen		

37.3 **Reflexive pronoun or *each other***
(Reflexivpronomen oder *each other*)

wir ... uns		→	***ourselves***
ihr ... euch	selbst	→	***yourselves***
sie ... sich		→	***themselves***

wir ... uns			
ihr ... euch	gegenseitig	→	***each other***
sie ... sich			

They watched themselves on the video.
Sie sahen sich (selbst) auf dem Video an.

They looked at each other and smiled.
Sie sahen sich (gegenseitig) an ... / Sie sahen einander an ...

Statt *each other* wird auch *one another* verwendet:
*They looked at **one another** and smiled.*

*Wo brauchst du ein Reflexivpronomen? Wo brauchst du **kein** Reflexivpronomen? Wo brauchst du* each other?

1 We're going to meet ... in the park after school.
2 He hurt ... and had to sit ... down for a moment.
3 We talked to ... on the phone yesterday.
4 People who talk to ... are a bit scary, I think.
5 Come on, we have to hurry ... or we'll be late. – Relax ...! We've got plenty of time!
6 I don't need your help. I can help ... .

37.4 ***myself, yourself* etc. as emphasizing pronouns**
(*myself, yourself* usw. als verstärkende Pronomen)

We were able to talk to **the director** himself.
Wir konnten mit dem Regisseur selbst sprechen.

The room itself was OK, but the view was horrible.
Das Zimmer selbst war OK, ...

Do you like the poster? **I** designed it myself.
Magst du das Poster? Ich habe es selbst entworfen.

It'll be a lot cheaper if **we** paint the room ourselves.
Es ist viel billiger, wenn wir das Zimmer selbst streichen.

myself, yourself usw. werden auch verwendet, um ein Nomen oder Pronomen hervorzuheben oder um zu betonen, dass jemand etwas allein, ohne Hilfe getan hat. Im Deutschen verwenden wir „selbst" oder „selber".

They've painted the room themselves.

The adjective (Das Adjektiv)

38 **Use (Gebrauch)**

Martin is happy. He got a new camera for his birthday. It looks expensive.
Martin ist glücklich. Er hat zum Geburtstag eine neue Kamera bekommen. Sie sieht teuer aus.

▶ *Adverb oder Adjektiv nach bestimmten Verben: 44*

Adjektive werden verwendet, um **Eigenschaften** oder **Merkmale** von Personen, Sachen, Begriffen usw. zu beschreiben. Adjektive stehen vor einen Nomen oder nach bestimmten Verben *(be, become, get, look, seem, sound, taste, …)*.

39 **Comparison (Steigerung)**

	Komparativ (Comparative)	Superlativ (Superlative)
clean	clean**er**	clean**est**
big	bigg**er**	bigg**est**
happy	happi**er**	happi**est**
useful	more useful	most useful
famous	more famous	most famous
expensive	more expensive	most expensive
difficult	more difficult	most difficult
good	better	best
bad	worse	worst
much/many	more	most
(a) little	less	least

- Steigerung mit *-er/-est*:
  - **einsilbige** Adjektive
  - **zweisilbige** Adjektive, die auf **-y** enden
- Steigerung mit *more/most*:
  - die meisten **zweisilbigen** Adjektive, die <u>nicht</u> auf **-y** enden
  - Adjektive mit **mehr als zwei Silben**
- **unregelmäßige** Steigerung:
  - *good, bad*
  - *much/many, (a) little*

Additional information

clever	clever**er**/**more** clever	clever**est**/**most** clever
simple	simpl**er**/**more** simple	simpl**est**/**most** simple

Where's the **nearest** bus stop.   nächstgelegen (räumlich)
I have to get off at the **next** stop.   nächstfolgend

Shakira's **latest** CD is better   neueste, jüngste CD
than her **last** one.   letzte CD („die davor")

- Manche zweisilbigen Adjektive können mit *-er/-est* oder *more/most* gesteigert werden; Beispiele: *clever, simple, stupid.*
- *near* und *late* haben zwei Superlativ-Formen mit verschiedenen Bedeutungen. (Im Zweifelsfall muss man die Steigerungs-formen eines Adjektivs in einem guten Wörterbuch nachschlagen.)

40 **The adjective in comparisons (Das Adjektiv in Vergleichen)**

Lilly is as **tall** as Jacob.

Jacob is not as **tall** as Olivia.

Olivia is **tall**er than him.
⚠ taller than me/him/...
(*not:* ... than ~~I/he/...~~)

Olivia is the **tall**est.

- *as ... as* („so ... wie")
- *not as ... as* („nicht so ... wie")
- **Komparativ** (1. Steigerungsform) + *than*: *taller than* („größer **als**")
- *the* + **Superlativ** (2. Steigerungsform): *the tallest* („der/die größte, am größten")

The adverb (Das Adverb)

41 Forms (Formen)

> always, often, sometimes, now, then, today, soon, still, here, there, up, down, perhaps, very, quite, too, ...
>
> badly, easily, happily, politely, quietly, terribly, usually, generally, finally, luckily, ...
>
> fast, hard, high, late, long, early, daily, ...

Es gibt verschiedene Arten von Adverbien:

- „ursprüngliche" Adverbien (= Adverbien, die nicht von Adjektiven abgeleitet sind)
- Adverbien, die **von Adjektiven abgeleitet** sind (durch Anhängen von **-ly**)
- Adverbien, die **dieselbe Form wie Adjektive** haben

K Grandpa always drives carefully.   ... fährt immer **vorsichtig**.

Grandpa is always very careful. ... ist immer sehr **vorsichtig**.

! Im Deutschen haben Adverbien der Art und Weise und Adjektive dieselbe Form. Im Englischen in der Regel nicht.

! Jessica is a **good** guitar player. She plays the guitar well.

Das Adverb zum Adjektiv **good** heißt **well**.

► *Stellung der verschiedenen Arten von Adverbien: 6*

42 Use (Gebrauch)

1 Grandpa **drives** carefully, especially at night.
Opa fährt vorsichtig, ...

2 He thinks driving at night is terribly **dangerous**.
... schrecklich gefährlich

3 My sister Emma always drives really **fast**.
... wirklich schnell

4 Emma nearly had an accident last week.
Luckily, **she was able to stop the car in time.**
Glücklicherweise konnte sie das Auto rechtzeitig zum Stehen bringen.

Adverbien können sich

(1) auf ein **Verb** beziehen. Sie geben dann an, wie etwas geschieht oder wie etwas getan wird, und werden **Adverb der Art und Weise** *(adverb of manner)* genannt.

(2) auf ein **Adjektiv** beziehen.

(3) auf ein **anderes Adverb** beziehen.

(4) Satzadverbien *(sentence adverbs)* beziehen sich auf den **ganzen Satz**.

43 Comparison (Steigerung)

fast	fast**er**	fast**est**
early	earli**er**	earli**est**
carefully	more **carefully**	most **carefully**
quickly	more **quickly**	most **quickly**
often	more **often**	most **often**
well	better	best
badly	worse	worst
much	more	most
little	less	least

- Steigerung mit **-er/-est**: **einsilbige** Adverbien und **early**
- Steigerung mit **more/most**:
  – Adverbien **auf -ly** (außer *early*)
  – andere **mehrsilbige** Adverbien
- **unregelmäßige** Steigerung:
  – **well, badly**
  – **much, little**

44 Adverb or adjective after certain verbs? (Adverb oder Adjektiv nach bestimmten Verben?) 3:5

Tätigkeit: verb + adverb	Zustand, Eigenschaft: verb + adjective
She **shouted** angrily at me. Sie schrie mich wütend an.	She **felt** angry. Sie fühlte sich wütend.
The choir **sang** beautifully. Der Chor sang wunderschön.	The song **sounded** beautiful. Das Lied klang wunderschön.
He **looked round** nervously. Er sah sich nervös um.	He **looked** nervous. Er sah nervös aus.
We were all **talking** excitedly. Wir redeten alle aufgeregt durcheinander.	They **seemed** excited. Sie schienen aufgeregt zu sein.

■ **Adverbien der Art und Weise** beziehen sich auf Verben und drücken aus, wie eine **Tätigkeit** ausgeführt wird („wie jemand etwas <u>tut</u>").

■ Einige Verben beschreiben nicht Tätigkeiter, sondern **Zustände** oder **Eigenschaften** („wie jemand oder etwas <u>ist</u>"). Nach solchen Verben stehen **Adjektive**. (Man erkennt diese Verben daran, dass sie durch *be* ersetzt werden können.)

(to) **be**	sein	(to) **feel**	sich (an)fühlen
(to) **become**	werden	(to) **look**	aussehen
(to) **get**	werden	(to) **smell**	riechen; stinken
(to) **seem**	(zu sein) scheinen	(to) **sound**	klingen
(to) **stay**	bleiben	(to) **taste**	schmecken

Dies sind die wichtigsten Verben, nach denen **Adjektive** stehen.

1 They **looked** nervously into the box.   schauen, sehen
   He **smelled** the flowers happily.   an etwas riechen
   The cook **tasted** the soup carefully.   probieren, kosten

2 They **looked** scared.   aussehen
   The flowers **smelled** wonderful.   riechen; stinken
   The soup **tasted** delicious.   schmecken

! Bei den Verben *look, smell* und *taste* kann – je nach Bedeutung – ein Adverb oder ein Adjektiv stehen:
(1) Ein **Adverb** steht, wenn eine **Tätigkeit** beschrieben wird.
(2) Ein **Adjektiv** steht, wenn ein **Zustand** oder eine **Eigenschaft** beschrieben wird.

*They thought they sang beautifully,
but it sounded just awful.*

Adverb oder Adjektiv? Vervollständige die Sätze mit der richtigen Form der Wörter in den Klammern.

1 (careful / happy)   I picked up the little boy ... . He smiled at me ... .
2 (tired / good)   You look ... . Didn't you sleep ...?
3 (difficult / easy)   The exercise seemed ... at first, but we were able do it ... in the end.
4 (awful / horrible)   I think dog food smells ... . I'm sure it tastes ... too.
5 (nice / usual)   If you ask ..., people will ... help you.
6 (slow / clear)   Although he tried to speak ..., his voice didn't sound very ... .
7 (great / good)   She felt ... . She was sure she had done ... in the test.

Prepositions (Präpositionen)

45   **Use (Gebrauch)**

among the
brown frogs

onto the car

on the car

up the
tree

into the car

in/inside the car

down the tree

out of the car

off the car

in front of the car

Präpositionen des Ortes und der Richtung

Präpositionen (Verhältniswörter) können aus einem Wort bestehen *(in, at)* oder aus mehreren Wörtern *(in front of, out of)*.
Sie drücken Beziehungen zwischen Dingen, Personen oder Ereignissen aus. Diese Beziehungen können **räumlicher** (Ort, Richtung), **zeitlicher** (Zeitpunkt, Zeitraum, Reihenfolge) oder **anderer Art** sein.

- at, behind, between, in, in front of, next to, under, ...
  away from, into, on, out of, through, under, up, ...

- after, at, before, between, for, in, on, past, since, till, ...

- about, for, from, in, of, on, like, with, without, ...

Präpositionen lassen sich einteilen in

- Präpositionen des **Ortes** und der **Richtung**

- Präpositionen der **Zeit**

- **sonstige** Präpositionen.

Ort	in Spain; in the photo	in Spanien; auf dem Foto
Zeit	in April; in the evening	im April; am Abend
sonstig	in English	auf Englisch

Präpositionen können verschiedene Verhältnisse kennzeichnen – und dabei verschiedene Entsprechungen haben.

Have you **talked** to Sarah about the party yet?
Are you **interested** in art?
What's the **difference** between these CD players?

Präpositionen können mit anderen Wörtern (Verben, Adjektiven, Nomen) fest verbunden sein.

! Beachte die **Endstellung der Präposition** in

1   Who were you **talking** to?   Mit wem ...?
    What were you **talking** about?   Worüber/Über was ...?

(1)   **Fragesätzen** mit *who, what* usw.

2   They wanted to know what we were **talking** about.
    ..., worüber/über was wir geredet haben.

(2)   **indirekten Fragen**

3   I know the woman that you were **talking** to.
    ... die Frau, mit der du geredet hast.

(3)   **Relativsätzen**

4   Grandpa needs someone to **talk** to.
    ... jemanden, mit dem er reden kann.

(4)   **Infinitivkonstruktionen**

5   Their decision was **talked** about for weeks.
    Über ihre Entscheidung wurde wochenlang geredet.

(5)   **Passivsätzen**.

Conditional sentences (Bedingungssätze)

46 **Overview (Übersicht)** 3 : 2 / 4 : 2

Nebensatz mit *if (if-clause)*	Hauptsatz *(Main clause)*
If it stays dry, Wenn es trocken bleibt,	we'll play football in the park. spielen wir Fußball im Park / werden wir Fußball … spielen.
Bedingung: *„Wenn …,"*	Folge: *„dann …"*

We'll play football in the park if it stays dry.

Bedingungssätze („Wenn …, dann …"-Sätze) bestehen aus einem **Nebensatz mit *if*** („wenn", „falls") und einem **Hauptsatz**. Im Nebensatz steht eine Bedingung. Der Hauptsatz beschreibt, was geschieht, wenn diese Bedingung erfüllt ist.

Der Hauptsatz kann auch vor dem *if*-Satz stehen. Es steht dann kein Komma!

Es gibt **drei Grundtypen**:

Type 1 – about the present or the future

After the first half of the race …

Mark   Allen

If Allen overtakes Mark, he will win the race.
Wenn Allen Mark überholt, gewinnt er das Rennen / wird er … gewinnen.

- **Typ 1**
  „Was ist, wenn …"
  (erfüllbare Bedingung)
  Die Mädchen halten es
  für gut möglich, dass
  Allen es schafft, Mark zu
  überholen. Die Hälfte
  des Rennens liegt ja
  noch vor den beiden.
  ▶ *Typ 1: 47*

Type 2 – about the present or the future

The race is almost over …

If Allen overtook Mark now, he would win.
Wenn Allen Mark jetzt überholen würde, würde er gewinnen.

- **Typ 2**
  „Was wäre, wenn …"
  (kaum oder wahrscheinlich nicht erfüllbare
  Bedingung)
  Die Mädchen halten es
  für unwahrscheinlich,
  dass Allen Mark noch
  überholt. Das Rennen
  ist ja so gut wie vorbei.
  ▶ *Typ 2: 48*

Type 3 – about the past

The race is over – Mark has won …

If he had overtaken Mark, Allen would have won.
Wenn er Mark überholt hätte , hätte Allen gewonnen.

- **Typ 3**
  **„Was wäre gewesen,
  wenn …"** (nicht mehr
  erfüllbare Bedingung)
  Das Rennen ist vorbei,
  Mark hat gewonnen.
  Die Mädchen reden nur
  darüber, was gewesen
  wäre, wenn …
  ▶ *Typ 3: 49*

47 Conditional sentences, type 1 (Bedingungssätze, Typ 1)

3 : 2 / 4 : 2

if-clause	Main clause
If Jamie leaves now,	he'll be home in time for the news.
If the rain doesn't stop,	we can't have a picnic.
If Grandma phones,	tell her I might be late.

simple present

- **will-future**
- **modal auxiliary** *(can/might/...)* **+ infinitive**
- **imperative**

Bedingungssatz 1 („Was <u>ist</u>, wenn …?"):
Im *if*-Satz *simple present*.

▶ *Andere Verbformen im if-Satz: 50*

If you add blue to yellow, you get green.
Wenn (Immer wenn) man blau zu gelb hinzugibt, erhält man grün.

Bedingungssätze vom Typ 1 beziehen sich auf die **Gegenwart** oder die **Zukunft**.

Der Sprecher nimmt an, dass die im *if*-Satz genannte Bedingung erfüllt werden kann: Es ist möglich oder wahrscheinlich, dass Jamie jetzt aufbricht, dass es weiterregnet, dass Oma anruft.
Der Hauptsatz beschreibt, was geschehen wird/kann/soll …, wenn die Bedingung erfüllt wird.

Der *if*-Satz steht in der Regel im *simple present*. Im Hauptsatz stehen meist das *will*-future, ein Modalverb + Infinitiv oder ein Imperativ.

In allgemein gültigen Aussagen („wenn etwas immer so ist") steht auch im Hauptsatz das *simple present*.

48 Conditional sentences, type 2 (Bedingungssätze, Typ 2)

3 : 2 / 4 : 2

if-clause	Main clause
If I had more money,	I'd travel (= I would travel) round the world.
If Amy was older,	she could stay out later.
If you kept quiet,	you might hear what I'm saying.

simple past

would/could/might + infinitive

Bedingungssatz 2 („Was <u>wäre</u>, wenn …?"):
Im *if*-Satz *simple past* (! nicht ~~would~~).

▶ *Andere Verbformen im if-Satz: 50*

K If I found $100 in the street, …   *(not:* If I ~~would find~~ …)
   … fände / finden würde …

If I were you, I wouldn't wait for them.
Wenn ich du wäre, würde ich … / An deiner Stelle würde ich …

Mit **Bedingungssätzen vom Typ 2** spekuliert der Sprecher darüber, was unter bestimmten Bedingungen jetzt oder in Zukunft geschehen würde oder geschehen könnte.

Die im *if*-Satz genannte Bedingung kann nicht erfüllt werden (Amy ist nun mal nicht älter), oder der Sprecher hält es für unwahrscheinlich, dass die Bedingung erfüllt wird.

Der *if*-Satz steht in der Regel im *simple past*. Im Hauptsatz stehen *would/could/ might* + Infinitiv.

! Im *if*-Satz darf kein *would* stehen. Im deutschen „wenn"-Satz verwenden wir oft „würde", aber im englischen *if*-Satz steht das *simple past*.

Ratschläge werden im Englischen oft mit *If I were you …* eingeleitet.

*Was trifft zu, **A** oder **B**?*

1 If it wasn't raining, we could go surfing.   **A** it's raining   **B** it might rain
2 If he's late again, Dan will be in trouble.   **A** he is late   **B** he might be late
3 Can you close the windows if it rains?   **A** it's raining   **B** it might rain
4 If Mum calls, tell her I'll be home by 10.   **A** Mum won't call   **B** Mum might call
5 If the lights were on, we'd know he's in.   **A** the lights aren't on   **B** the lights might be on
6 He'd be so happy if he had a dog.   **A** he doesn't have a dog **B** he might have a dog

49   **Conditional sentences, type 3**
(Bedingungssätze, Typ 3)   4: 2

if-clause	Main clause

If she had phoned,   I'd have met her at the station.
Wenn sie angerufen hätte, hätte ich sie am Bahnhof abgeholt.
If it had been warmer, we could have gone swimming.
Wenn es wärmer gewesen wäre, hätten wir … gehen können.
If he had kept quiet,   Mr Stone mightn't have given him
                        extra homework.
Wenn er still gewesen wäre, hätte ihm Mr Stone vielleicht keine
zusätzlichen Hausaufgaben aufgegeben.

past perfect   ***would have / could have / might have***
                        + past participle

   Bedingungssatz 3 („Was <u>wäre gewesen</u>, wenn …?"):
                       Im *if*-Satz *past perfect*.

! If she'd phoned,   = had phoned
       I'd have met her at the station.   = would have met

If I had worked harder at school, I might be a doctor now.
Wenn ich … härter gearbeitet hätte, wäre ich jetzt vielleicht Arzt.

If Daniel hadn't borrowed my bike, I'd be able to go on a
bike tour with Ella at the weekend.
… könnte ich am Wochenende eine Radtour mit Ella machen.

Bedingungssätze vom Typ 3 beziehen sich
auf die **Vergangenheit**, d.h., sie kommentieren eine Situation, die schon vorbei ist.
Der Sprecher stellt sich vor, was unter
bestimmten Bedingungen hätte geschehen
können (aber eben nicht passiert ist).

Wir wissen, dass die im *if*-Satz genannte
Bedingung nicht eingetreten ist:
Sie hat nicht angerufen (und ich habe sie
deshalb nicht abgeholt), es war nicht
wärmer (und wir sind nicht schwimmen
gegangen), er war nicht still (und hat daher
zusätzliche Aufgaben bekommen).

Der *if*-Satz steht im *past perfect*.
Im Hauptsatz stehen *would have/
could have/might have* + Partizip Perfekt.

! Achtung:
had im *if*-Satz und *would* im **Hauptsatz**
können beide zu *'d* verkürzt werden.

Im Hauptsatz kann auch *would/could/
might* + Infinitiv stehen. Dann beschreibt
der Hauptsatz, was jetzt oder zukünftig der
Fall wäre, wenn die Begingung in der
Vergangenheit erfüllt worden wäre.

Sieh dir das Beispiel an und bilde Bedingungssätze vom Typ 3.

1 We couldn't go shopping. The shops were all closed.   *If the shops hadn't been closed,*
                                                            we could have gone shopping.
2 Claire didn't turn off her computer, so it was on all night.   *If Claire had turned off …*
3 I found out about the murders when I turned on the radio.   *If I hadn't turned on …*
4 Mr Johnson's car radio was stolen. He hadn't locked his car.   *If he had …*
5 The weather wasn't good enough, so we couldn't go swimming.   *If the weather …*

50 **Other verb forms in the *if*-clause**
(Andere Verbformen im *if*-Satz)

If I can help you, I will.   Wenn ich dir helfen kann, ...

If I could help you, I would.   Wenn ich dir helfen könnte, ...

Sorry. If you're having lunch now, I'll call back later.
Wenn Sie gerade zu Mittag essen, ...

If Ella has missed the bus, we'll have to start without her.
Wenn Ella den Bus verpasst hat, ...

If they were working now, the lights would be on.
Wenn sie jetzt arbeiteten/arbeiten würden, ...

Je nach Situation können auch andere
Verbformen im *if*-Satz vorkommen.

Relative clauses (Relativsätze)

51 **Use (Gebrauch)**   3: 3 / 4: 5

I'm looking for a **shop** that sells locally grown fruit.
Ich suche ein Geschäft, das Obst hier aus der Gegend verkauft.

Who's that over there?
– That's the **boy** who I met in Bristol last month.
... der Junge, den ich letzten Monat in Bristol kennengelernt habe.

Relativsätze beziehen sich auf ein **Nomen**.
Sie **bestimmen dieses Nomen** genauer:
Erst durch den Relativsatz wissen wir,
wer oder was genau gemeint ist.
(Daher werden solche Relativsätze <u>bestim-
mende</u> oder auch <u>notwendige</u> Relativsätze
– englisch *defining relative clauses* –
genannt.)

▶ *Nicht bestimmende Relativsätze: 55*

K
	S	V	O
The woman	who	helped	us ...

Die Frau, die uns geholfen hat, ...

! In diesen Relativsätzen steht kein Komma,
und wie in allen englischen Nebensätzen
gilt auch in Relativsätzen die Wortstellung
S – V – O.

▶ *Wortstellung in Nebensätzen: 4*

52 **The relative pronouns (Die Relativpronomen)** 3: 3 / 4: 5

52.1 ***who, which, that***

Do you know the **boys** who/that stole your bike?
Kennst du die Jungen, die dein Rad gestohlen haben?

Do you know a **café** which/that is open at night?
Kennen Sie ein Café, das nachts geöffnet hat?

- Für **Personen** wird *who*, manchmal auch
  that verwendet:
  *the man/woman/people **who/that** ...*

- Für **Dinge (und Tiere)** wird *which* oder
  that verwendet:
  *the house/bag/animals **which/that** ...*

52.2 ***whose ...***

Are those the **girls** whose parents are from Trinidad?
... die Mädchen, deren Eltern ...

This is a **school** whose students always get good results.
... eine Schule, deren Schüler und Schülerinnen ...

- Das Relativpronomen *whose* („dessen",
  „deren") bezieht sich meist auf Personen,
  wird aber auch für Dinge und Tiere
  benutzt.

53 Relative clauses with *which* to refer to a whole clause (Satzbezogene Relativsätze mit *which*) 4:5

Her son hasn't phoned, which is very worrying.
Ihr Sohn hat nicht angerufen, **was** sehr beunruhigend ist.

Our neighbours helped us to tidy up after the party, which I think was very good of them.
..., **was** ich sehr nett von ihnen fand.

In 1980, John Lennon was murdered, which shocked Beatles fans all over the world.
..., **was** Beatles-Fans auf der ganzen Welt schockierte.

Relativsätze mit **which** können sich auch **auf einen ganzen Satz beziehen**: Sie kommentieren dann die Aussage des Hauptsatzes.

! Satzbezogene Relativsätze werden durch Komma abgetrennt.

Im Deutschen werden solche Relativsätze mit „was" eingeleitet.

a) Verwende einen Relativsatz, um die beiden Sätze zu kombinieren.

1 There are a couple of things on the kitchen table. I need them for the salad.
There are a couple of things on the kitchen table that I ...
2 A woman was taken to hospital last night. She's still unconscious.   *The woman who ...*
3 A girl saved a little boy from drowning. She got a medal.   *The girl ...*
4 John lent me a book. I lost it.   *I ...*

b) Welche Sätze passen zusammen? Verbinde sie mit which.

1 15-year-old Stevie won the 100 metres.
2 She called him silly and stupid.
3 Dad has given up smoking.
4 We're moving to Leeds in the summer.

A It means I'll have to change school.
B That will save him a lot of money.
C That was really rude of her.
D It surprised everybody.

54 Contact clauses (Relativsätze ohne Relativpronomen) 3:3

	Subject	Verb
1 I like boys	**who**	make me laugh.
Ich mag Jungen,	die	mich zum Lachen bringen.
I don't like films	**that**	last too long.
Ich mag Filme nicht,	die	zu lang sind.

	Object	Subject	Verb
2 Paul is a boy	who	**I**	like a lot.
Paul ist ein Junge,	den	**ich**	sehr gern mag.
Where's the DVD	which	**Dan**	lent you?
Wo ist die DVD,	die	**Dan**	dir geliehen hat?

Das Relativpronomen kann **Subjekt** oder **Objekt** sein:

(1) In diesen Sätzen sind die Relativpronomen **Subjekt** des Relativsatzes. Sie stehen <u>direkt vor dem Verb</u>.

(2) Hier sind die Relativpronomen Objekt des Relativsatzes.

Paul is a boy _____ I like a lot.
Paul ist ein Junge, den **ich** sehr gern mag.
Where's the DVD _____ **Dan** lent you?
Wo ist die DVD, die **Dan** dir geliehen hat?
Cornwall is one of most beautiful regions _____ I know.
Cornwall ist eine der schönsten Regionen, die ich kenne.

Wenn das Relativpronomen Objekt des Relativsatzes ist, wird es meist **weggelassen**. Das ist im Deutschen nicht möglich.

Relativsätze ohne Relativpronomen nennt man **contact clauses**.

Is that the train which goes to Cornwall?

(*not*: Is that ~~the train goes to Cornwall~~?)

Vorsicht! Wenn das **Relativpronomen direkt vor dem Verb** steht, ist es Subjekt – dann darf es **nicht wegfallen**!

K
or Who's the girl **that** Paul is talking to?
Who's the girl ☐ Paul is talking to?
Wer ist das Mädchen, mit dem Paul redet?

What's the name of the family you stayed with?
Wie heißt die Familie, bei der ihr gewohnt habt?

The concert I told **you** about is sold out.
Das Konzert, von dem ich **dir** erzählt habe, ist ausverkauft.

Beachte die Stellung der Präposition in Relativsätzen.

In welchen Sätzen kann das Relativpronomen wegfallen?
Schreibe die Sätze als contact clauses *in dein Heft.*

1 Have you kept in touch with that girl **that** you met in Spain?
2 Mum, the woman **who** phoned yesterday has just called again.
3 I've found the CD **that** you've been looking for.
4 The hotel **which** we stayed at was really nice, but quite expensive too.
5 Where's that book **that** John sent from England?
6 The boy **who** won the 100 metres is only 15 years old.

Additional information

55

**Non-defining relative clauses
(Nicht bestimmende Relativsätze)**   4:5

Charlie Chaplin, **who was born in England,** made most of his films in Hollywood.
Charlie Chaplin, der in England geboren wurde, hat die meisten seiner Filme in Hollywood gedreht.

The film studios, **which we hadn't expected to be so big,** were one of the highlights of our tour.
Die Filmstudios, von denen wir nicht erwartet hatten, dass sie so groß sein würden, waren einer der Höhepunkte unserer Tour.

Astrid Lindgren, **whose 'Pippi Longstocking' has become world-famous,** was born in 1907 and died in Stockholm in 2002.
Astrid Lindgren, deren „Pippi Langstrumpf" Weltberühmtheit erlangte, wurde 1907 geboren und starb im Jahre 2002 in Stockholm.

Nicht bestimmende Relativsätze kommen hauptsächlich in geschriebenem Englisch vor. Sie geben **Zusatzinformationen**, die man nicht unbedingt braucht, um zu verstehen, von wem oder was die Rede ist:
Man versteht den Satz
Charlie Chaplin made most of his films in Hollywood
auch ohne den Relativsatz
who was born in England.

Beachte:
- In nicht bestimmten Relativsätzen darf das Relativpronomen <u>nie</u> weggelassen werden.
- Es können nur die Relativpronomen **who, which** und **whose** verwendet werden – nicht aber **that**.
- Nicht bestimmte Relativsätze werden durch Kommas abgetrennt.

Indirect speech (Indirekte Rede)

56 **Direct and indirect speech**
(Direkte und indirekte Rede)

3:4 / 4:2

> I can't lend you
> my bike, Robert.

Direct speech	Asif says, 'I can't lend you my bike, Robert.' Asif sagt: „Ich kann dir mein Rad nicht leihen, Robert."
Indirect speech	Asif says (that) he can't lend Robert his bike. Asif sagt, dass er Robert sein Rad nicht leihen kann.

Man kann direkt oder indirekt wiedergeben, was jemand sagt (oder gesagt hat).

■ In der **direkten Rede** gibt man **wörtlich** wieder, was jemand sagt, schreibt oder denkt. Direkte Rede steht in der Regel in Anführungszeichen.

■ In der **indirekten Rede** (*indirect speech* oder *reported speech*) berichtet man, was jemand sagt, schreibt oder denkt. Die indirekte Rede wird mit Verben wie *say, tell sb., add, answer, explain, think, write, ask, want to know* eingeleitet.

! Im Englischen steht vor der indirekten Rede **kein Komma**.
Die Konjunktion *that* („dass") wird oft weggelassen, besonders nach *say, tell, think*.

Direct speech	*Asif* 'I can't lend you my bike, Robert.'
Indirect speech	
1 *(Robert reports)*	Asif says he can't lend me his bike.
2 *(his dad reports)*	Asif says he can't lend Robert his bike.

Wie im Deutschen werden in der indirekten Rede die Pronomen und Possessivbegleiter angepasst – je nachdem, wer wem berichtet.
▶ *Veränderungen von Orts- und Zeitangaben: 61*

57 **Indirect speech: reporting verb in the *simple present***
(Indirekte Rede: einleitendes Verb im *simple present*)

Direct speech	*Ella* 'We usually get up at 7.15.'
Indirect speech	She says they usually get up at 7.15.
Direct speech	*Aidan* 'I'm really enjoying our trip.'
Indirect speech	We got a postcard from Aidan today. He says that he's enjoying his trip.

Wenn das einleitende Verb im **simple present** steht *(she says)*, bleibt die Zeitform der direkten Rede unverändert.

58 **Indirect speech: reporting verb in the *simple past***
(Indirekte Rede: einleitendes Verb im *simple past*)

Direct speech	*Jody* 'My name is Jody.'
Indirect speech	She said her name was Jody. Sie sagte, ihr Name sei/ist Jody.
Direct speech	*Noah* 'I haven't seen *Batman* yet.'
Indirect speech	Noah told me last week that he hadn't seen *Batman* yet.

Wenn das einleitende Verb im **simple past** steht *(she said, he told me)*, werden in der indirekten Rede meist andere Zeitformen verwendet als in der direkten Rede:
Die Zeitformen der direkten Rede werden **um eine Zeitstufe in die Vergangenheit „zurückverschoben"** *(backshift of tenses)*.
▶ *Backshift of tenses (Übersicht): siehe S. 63*

Veränderungen der Zeitform bei einleitendem Verb im *simple past (backshift of tenses)*

		Direct speech	Indirect speech
present ►	past	'Philip is German.' 'We play cards on Fridays.' 'I'm waiting for my dad.'	She said that Philip was German. They told us they played cards on Fridays. She said she was waiting for her dad.
past ►	past perfect	'It was a great trip.' 'I met my wife at a dance.' 'We were watching TV.'	They agreed it had been a great trip. He told me he had met his wife at a dance. She added that they had been watching TV.
present perfect ►	past perfect	'I haven't been to Bath yet.' 'Olivia has found a job.' 'They've been working.'	I explained that I hadn't been to Bath yet. He said that Olivia had found a job. She answered that they had been working.
will-future ►	would + infinitive	'I'll phone him.'	She promised she'd phone him.
going to-future ►	was/were going to + infinitive	'I'm going to work harder.'	I said I was going to work harder.

Indirekte Rede mit einleitendem Verb im *simple past*

Die Zeitform der direkten Rede wird um eine Stufe in die Vergangenheit zurückverschoben:

<u>Present</u> forms ► <u>Past</u> forms
<u>Past</u> forms ► <u>Past perfect</u> forms

Direct speech **Indirect speech**	*Sophie* 'The bus had already left.' Sophie said the bus had already left.
Direct speech **Indirect speech**	*Oliver* 'I met my wife at a dance.' Oliver said he met his wife at a dance.
Direct speech **Indirect speech**	*Grace* 'Cardiff is in Wales.' She said Cardiff is / was in Wales.
Direct speech **Indirect speech**	*Luke* 'Andrew has a cold.' He said Andrew has / had a cold.

! Beachte:

- Verben im *past perfect* bleiben unverändert, da man sie nicht noch weiter „zurückverschieben" kann.
- Verben im *simple past* werden in der Umgangssprache oft <u>nicht</u> ins *past perfect* verändert.

Die Zeitform der direkten Rede kann auch dann unverändert bleiben,

- wenn die Aussage allgemein gültig ist

- wenn die Aussage zum Zeitpunkt des Berichtens immer noch zutrifft (*hier*: Andrew ist immer noch erkältet).

Berichte, was sie gesagt haben. Schreib die Aussagen in indirekter Rede in dein Heft.

(1) *Colin* 'Chris Martin from *Coldplay* is my favourite singer.'
(2) *Julie* '*Coldplay* are giving a free open-air concert in June.'
(3) *Emily* 'I've never been to an open-air concert.'
(4) *Mark* 'I don't like open-air concerts.'
(5) *Colin* 'I think they're great fun.'

(1) *Colin told me that Chris Martin …*   2) *Julie said …*

59   **Questions in indirect speech**
(Fragen in der indirekten Rede)   4: 2

Direct speech	*Lilly* '**How** do you like Florida?'
Indirect speech	Lilly asked me **how** I liked Florida. / Lilly wanted to know **how** I liked Florida.

Indirekte Fragen werden z.B. mit *ask, want to know* und *wonder* eingeleitet. Wenn diese einleitenden Verben im *simple past* stehen, gelten die Regeln für die Veränderung der Zeitformen *(backshift of tenses)*.

▶ *Backshift of tenses (Übersicht): siehe S. 63*

Direct speech	*Lilly* '**When** did you arrive?'
Indirect speech	She also wanted to know **when** I had arrived.

Direct speech	*Lilly* '**Do** you like surfing?'
Indirect speech	She asked me if I liked surfing. / She asked me whether I liked surfing.

Handelt es sich bei der direkten Frage um eine **Entscheidungsfrage** *(yes/no question)*, dann wird die indirekte Frage mit **if** oder **whether** („ob") eingeleitet.

Excuse me, **can you tell me** when the museum opens? / Excuse me, **I'd like to know** when the museum opens.

Do you know if the match has started yet?

Indirekte Fragen werden oft verwendet, um höflich um Auskunft zu bitten, z.B.

   Can you tell me …? + indirekte Frage
   Do you know …? + indirekte Frage
   I'd like to know … + indirekte Frage.

a) Mr Brown arbeitet an einem Fahrkartenschalter. In der Pause erzählt er einem Kollegen, welche Fragen er beantworten musste. – Was berichtet er seinem Kollegen?

1	*(A girl)* 'Can you look after my surfboard for a while?'	*A girl asked me if I …*
2	*(A little boy)* 'Do I need a ticket for my teddy bear?'	*A little boy wondered if he …*
3	*(A woman)* 'Where's the nearest internet café, please?'	*A woman …*

b) Bitte höflich um Auskunft.

1	'Where can I park my car?'	*Can you tell me where I …?*
2	'How long does it take to get to Bath?'	*Excuse me, I'd like to know …*
3	'When does the post office open?'	*Do you know …?*

60 **Commands and requests in indirect speech**
(Aufforderungen u. Bitten in der indirekten Rede) 4: 2

(1) Ryan, take the cameras into the garden.

(2) Eve, don't let the reporters in.

(3) Jack, could you open a window, please?

(4) Sophia, please don't forget the spotlights.

1 He told Ryan **to take** the cameras into the garden.
Er sagte Ryan, er solle die Kameras in den Garten bringen. /
Er forderte Ryan auf, die Kameras in den Garten zu bringen.

2 He told Eve **not to let** the reporters in.
Er sagte Eve, dass sie die Reporter nicht hereinlassen soll.

3 He asked Jack **to open** a window.
Er bat Jack, ein Fenster zu öffnen.

4 He asked Sophia **not to forget** the spotlights.
Er bat Sophia, nicht die Scheinwerfer zu vergessen.

Aufforderungen und **Bitten** werden in der indirekten Rede meist durch eine **Infinitivkonstruktion** wiedergegeben:

- Für die Wiedergabe von **Aufforderungen** verwendet man meist *tell sb. to do sth.* (bzw. *tell sb. not to do sth.*). (1, 2)

- Für die Wiedergabe von **Bitten** verwendet man meist *ask sb. to do sth.* (bzw. *ask sb. not to do sth.*). (3, 4)

Berichte, was die Lehrerin gesagt hat.

(1) Quiet!

(2) Listen, please.

(3) Tim, Dan – don't argue.

(4) Sue, Lucy – go and get the head teacher, please.

1   *Mrs Waller told us to ...*
2   *She asked us ...*
3   *She told Tim and Dan ...*
4   *She asked Sue and Lucy ...*

61 **Changes in adverbials of place and time**
(Veränderungen von Orts- und Zeitangaben)

Alex (on the phone from Spain)	'I like it a lot here.'
His father (to a friend)	Alex phoned from Spain. He **said** he liked it a lot there.
(On a postcard from Lucy)	I'm flying to Paris tomorrow.
Her mother (to a friend, a week later)	... and she **wrote** that she was flying to Paris the next day.

In der indirekten Rede werden – wie im Deutschen – die Orts- und Zeitangaben aus der Sicht des Berichtenden gewählt.
Sie können sich also, je nach Situation, gegenüber der direkten Rede verändern.

Short forms (Kurzformen)

62   **Overview (Übersicht)**

Beim Sprechen und in persönlichen Briefen werden meist **Kurzformen** verwendet.

be

I'm	I am	**here**'s	here is
you're	you are	**there**'s	there is
he's	he is	**what**'s	what is
she's	she is	**when**'s	when is
it's	it is	**where**'s	where is
we're	we are	**who**'s	who is
you're	you are	**how**'s	how is
they're	they are	**that**'s	that is

have

I've	I have	**I**'d	I had
you've	you have	**you**'d	you had
he's	he has	**he**'d	he had
she's	she has	**she**'d	she had
it's	it has	**it**'d	it had
we've	we have	**we**'d	we had
you've	you have	**you**'d	you had
they've	they have	**they**'d	they had

will / would

I'll	I will	**I**'d	I would
you'll	you will	**you**'d	you would
he'll	he will	**he**'d	he would
she'll	she will	**she**'d	she would
it'll	it will	**it**'d	it would
we'll	we will	**we**'d	we would
you'll	you will	**you**'d	you would
they'll	they will	**they**'d	they would

Hilfsverb + not

isn't	is not	**hasn**'t	has not	**don**'t	do not	**can**'t	cannot
aren't	are not	**haven**'t	have not	**doesn**'t	does not	**couldn**'t	could not
						mightn't	might not
wasn't	was not	**hadn**'t	had not	**didn**'t	did not	**mustn**'t	must not
weren't	were not					**needn**'t	need not
						shouldn't	should not
						won't	will not
						wouldn't	would not

Irregular verbs (Unregelmäßige Verben)

63 Overview (Übersicht)

Infinitive	Simple past form	Past participle	
(to) **be**	was/were	**been**	sein
(to) **beat**	beat	**beaten**	schlagen; besiegen
(to) **become**	became	**become**	werden
(to) **begin**	began	**begun**	beginnen, anfangen (mit)
(to) **bleed**	bled	**bled**	bluten
(to) **blow**	blew	**blown**	wehen, blasen, pusten
(to) **break** [eɪ]	broke	**broken**	(zer)brechen; kaputt machen; kaputt gehen
(to) **bring**	brought	**brought**	(mit-, her)bringen
(to) **broadcast**	broadcast	**broadcast**	ausstrahlen; senden
(to) **build**	built	**built**	bauen
(to) **buy**	bought	**bought**	kaufen
(to) **catch**	caught	**caught**	fangen; erwischen
(to) **choose** [uː]	chose [əʊ]	**chosen** [əʊ]	(aus)wählen; (sich) aussuchen
(to) **come**	came	**come**	kommen
(to) **cut**	cut	**cut**	schneiden
(to) **deal** with [iː]	dealt [e]	**dealt** [e]	sich beschäftigen mit
(to) **do**	did	**done** [ʌ]	tun, machen
(to) **draw**	drew	**drawn**	zeichnen
(to) **drink**	drank	**drunk**	trinken
(to) **drive** [aɪ]	drove	**driven** [ɪ]	*(ein Auto)* fahren
(to) **eat**	ate [et, eɪt]	**eaten**	essen
(to) **fall**	fell	**fallen**	(hin)fallen, stürzen
(to) **feed**	fed	**fed**	füttern
(to) **feel**	felt	**felt**	(sich) fühlen; sich anfühlen
(to) **fight**	fought	**fought**	kämpfen
(to) **find**	found	**found**	finden
(to) **fly**	flew	**flown**	fliegen
(to) **forget**	forgot	**forgotten**	vergessen
(to) **forgive**	forgave	**forgiven**	vergeben, verzeihen
(to) **get**	got	**got**	bekommen; holen; werden; (hin)kommen
(to) **give**	gave	**given**	geben
(to) **go**	went	**gone** [ɒ]	gehen, fahren
(to) **grow**	grew	**grown**	wachsen; anbauen, anpflanzen
(to) **hang**	hung	**hung**	*(etwas)* aufhängen
(to) **have (have got)**	had	**had**	haben, besitzen
(to) **hear** [ɪə]	heard [ɜː]	**heard** [ɜː]	hören
(to) **hide** [aɪ]	hid [ɪ]	**hidden** [ɪ]	(sich) verstecken
(to) **hit**	hit	**hit**	treffen; schlagen
(to) **hold**	held	**held**	halten
(to) **hurt**	hurt	**hurt**	wehtun; verletzen
(to) **keep**	kept	**kept**	(be)halten; aufbewahren
(to) **know** [nəʊ]	knew [njuː]	**known** [nəʊn]	wissen; kennen
(to) **lay** the table	laid	**laid**	den Tisch decken
(to) **lead** [iː]	led [e]	**led** [e]	führen
(to) **leave**	left	**left**	(weg)gehen; abfahren; verlassen; zurücklassen
(to) **lend**	lent	**lent**	(ver)leihen

Infinitive	Simple past form	Past participle	
(to) **let**	let	let	lassen
(to) **lie**	lay	lain	liegen
(to) **lose** [uː]	lost [ɒ]	lost [ɒ]	verlieren
(to) **make**	made	made	machen; bauen; bilden
(to) **mean** [iː]	meant [e]	meant [e]	bedeuten; meinen
(to) **meet**	met	met	(sich) treffen
(to) **pay**	paid	paid	bezahlen
(to) **put**	put	put	legen, stellen, *(wohin)* tun
(to) **read** [iː]	read [e]	read [e]	lesen
(to) **ride** [aɪ]	rode	ridden [ɪ]	reiten; *(Rad)* fahren
(to) **ring**	rang	rung	klingeln, läuten
(to) **rise** [aɪ]	rose	risen [ɪ]	(auf)steigen
(to) **run**	ran	run	rennen, laufen; verlaufen
(to) **say** [eɪ]	said [e]	said [e]	sagen
(to) **see**	saw	seen	sehen; besuchen, aufsuchen
(to) **sell**	sold	sold	verkaufen
(to) **send**	sent	sent	schicken, senden
(to) **set** a trap	set	set	eine Falle stellen
(to) **sew** [əʊ]	sewed [əʊ]	sewn [əʊ]	nähen
(to) **shake**	shook	shaken	schütteln
(to) **shine**	shone [ɒ]	shone [ɒ]	scheinen *(Sonne)*
(to) **shoot** [uː]	shot [ɒ]	shot [ɒ]	(er)schießen
(to) **show**	showed	shown	zeigen
(to) **shut** up	shut	shut	den Mund halten
(to) **sing**	sang	sung	singen
(to) **sit**	sat	sat	sitzen; sich setzen
(to) **sleep**	slept	slept	schlafen
(to) **speak**	spoke	spoken	sprechen
(to) **spend**	spent	spent	*(Zeit)* verbringen; *(Geld)* ausgeben
(to) **spit**	spat	spat	spucken
(to) **spread** [e]	spread [e]	spread [e]	(sich) ausbreiten, (sich) verbreiten
(to) **stand**	stood	stood	stehen; sich (hin)stellen
(to) **steal**	stole	stolen	stehlen
(to) **stick** on/out	stuck	stuck	aufkleben / herausragen, herausstehen
(to) **sweep**	swept	swept	fegen, kehren
(to) **swim**	swam	swum	schwimmen
(to) **take**	took	taken	nehmen; (weg-, hin)bringen; dauern, *(Zeit)* brauchen
(to) **teach**	taught	taught	unterrichten, lehren
(to) **tear** [eə]	tore [ɔː]	torn [ɔː]	(zer)reißen
(to) **tell**	told	told	erzählen, berichten
(to) **think**	thought	thought	denken, glauben, meinen
(to) **throw**	threw	thrown	werfen
(to) **understand**	understood	understood	verstehen
(to) **upset**	upset	upset	ärgern, kränken, aus der Fassung bringen
(to) **wake** up	woke	woken	aufwachen; wecken
(to) **wear** [eə]	wore [ɔː]	worn [ɔː]	tragen *(Kleidung)*
(to) **win**	won [ʌ]	won [ʌ]	gewinnen
(to) **write**	wrote	written	schreiben

Grammatical terms (Grammatische Begriffe)

English	German	Example
active ['æktɪv]	Aktiv	Toni **scored** the final goal.
adjective ['ædʒɪktɪv]	Adjektiv, Eigenschaftswort	good, big, red, expensive
adverb ['ædvɜːb]	Adverb, Umstandswort	
adverb of frequency ['friːkwənsi]	Adverb der Häufigkeit, Häufigkeitsadverb	always, often, never
adverb of indefinite time [ɪn'defɪnət]	Adverb der unbestimmten Zeit	already, ever, just, never
adverb of manner ['mænə]	Adverb der Art und Weise	badly, happily, well
adverbial [æd'vɜːbiəl]	Adverbial(bestimmung)	in Bristol; at ten o'clock
article ['ɑːtɪkl]	Artikel, Geschlechtswort	the; a/an
auxiliary (verb) [ɔːg'zɪliəri]	Hilfsverb	be, do, have; will, can, must
backshift of tenses ['bækʃɪft]	Rückverschiebung der Zeitform (indirekte Rede)	He said his name **was** Paul.
command [kə'mɑːnd]	Aufforderung(ssatz), Befehl(ssatz)	Be quiet. Don't talk.
comparison [kəm'pærɪsn]	Steigerung; Vergleich	old – older – oldest; as old as ... / older than ...
complement ['kɒmplɪmənt]	prädikative Ergänzung (zum Subjekt)	Reading is **fun**.
complex sentence ['kɒmpleks]	Satzgefüge (Verbindung aus Haupt- und Nebensatz)	I can't come because I'm ill.
conditional sentence [kən'dɪʃənl]	Bedingungssatz	If I knew it, I'd tell you.
conjunction [kən'dʒʌŋkʃn]	Konjunktion, Bindewort	and, or, ...; because, if, ...
contact clause ['kɒntækt klɔːz]	Relativsatz ohne Relativpronomen	You're the boy **I love**.
coordinating conjunction [kəʊ,ɔːdɪneɪtɪŋ kən'dʒʌŋkʃn]	nebenordnende Konjunktion, koordinierende Konjunktion	and, or, but, ...
countable noun ['kaʊntəbl]	zählbares Nomen	tree(s), idea(s), child(ren)
defining relative clause [dɪ'faɪnɪŋ]	bestimmender Relativsatz	The boy **who lives here** ...
definite article [,defɪnət_'ɑːtɪkl]	bestimmter Artikel	**the** [ðə] bag; **the** [ðɪ] apple
demonstrative determiner [dɪ,mɒnstrətɪv dɪ'tɜːmɪnə]	Demonstrativbegleiter, hinweisender Begleiter	this, that, these, those
demonstrative pronoun [dɪ,mɒnstrətɪv 'prəʊnaʊn]	Demonstrativpronomen, hinweisendes Fürwort	this, that, these, those
determiner [dɪ'tɜːmɪnə]	Begleiter	
direct speech [,daɪrekt 'spiːtʃ]	direkte Rede, wörtliche Rede	'My name is Paul.'
full verb	Vollverb (Wortart)	go, dance, see, work
future perfect [,fjuːtʃə 'pɜːfɪkt]	vollendete Zukunft, Futur II	Next July we **will have lived** here ten years.
gerund ['dʒerənd]	Gerundium	**Surfing** is fun.
going to-future	Futur mit going to	We**'re going to play** cards.
if-clause	Nebensatz mit if, if-Satz	**If I knew it**, I'd tell you.
imperative [ɪm'perətɪv]	Imperativ (Befehlsform)	Listen. Be quiet. Don't talk.
indefinite article [ɪn,defɪnət_'ɑːtɪkl]	unbestimmter Artikel	**a** bag; **an** apple
indirect speech ['ɪndərekt, 'ɪndaɪrekt]	indirekte Rede	He said his name was Paul.
infinitive [ɪn'fɪnətɪv]	Infinitiv (Grundform des Verbs)	(to) close, (to) see, (to) sit
irregular verb [ɪ,regjələ 'vɜːb]	unregelmäßiges Verb	(to) go – went – gone
main clause [meɪn]	Hauptsatz	If I knew it, **I'd tell you**.
main verb	Hauptverb, Vollverb (Teil des Prädikats)	I can **sing**. / We didn't **play**.
modal (auxiliary) [,məʊdl_ɔːg'zɪliəri]	modales Hilfsverb, Modalverb	can, could, must, may, will
negative statement [,negətɪv 'steɪtmənt]	verneinter Aussagesatz	I don't like bananas.
non-defining relative clause [dɪ'faɪnɪŋ]	nicht bestimmender Relativsatz	Schwarzenegger, **who was born in Austria,** later became a US governor.

noun [naʊn]	Nomen, Substantiv	*Dan, boy, sister, time*
object [ˈɒbdʒɪkt]	Objekt	*Jo is writing **a letter**.*
object form	Objektform (der Personalpronomen)	*me, you, him, her, it, us, …*
object question	Objektfrage, Frage nach dem Objekt	*Who did you talk to?*
of-**phrase** [ˈɒv freɪz]	*of*-Fügung	*the name **of the street***
part of speech [ˌpɑːt_əv ˈspiːtʃ] (= **word class**)	Wortart	
participle [ˈpɑːtɪsɪpl]	Partizip	*going, taking; gone, taken*
participle clause	Partizipialsatz	*The girl **waiting at the bus stop** is my sister.*
passive [ˈpæsɪv]	Passiv	*The final goal **was scored** by Toni.*
past participle [ˌpɑːst ˈpɑːtɪsɪpl]	Partizip Perfekt (3. Form des Verbs)	*gone, taken, watched*
past perfect [ˌpɑːst ˈpɜːfɪkt]	Plusquamperfekt, Vorvergangenheit	*He was late because he **had missed** the bus.*
past perfect progressive [ˌpɑːst ˌpɜːfɪkt prəˈgresɪv]	Verlaufsform des *past perfect*	*She **had been working** in the garden since 9 o'clock.*
past progressive [ˌpɑːst prəˈgresɪv]	Verlaufsform der Vergangenheit	*At 1.30 I **was having** lunch.*
personal passive [ˌpɜːsənl ˈpæsɪv]	persönliches Passiv	*She was offered a job.*
personal pronoun [ˌpɜːsənl ˈprəʊnaʊn]	Personalpronomen (persönliches Fürwort)	*I, you, he, she, it, we, …; me, you, him, her, it, us, …*
plural [ˈplʊərəl]	Plural, Mehrzahl	
positive statement [ˌpɒzətɪv ˈsteɪtmənt]	bejahter Aussagesatz	*I like oranges.*
possessive determiner [pəˌzesɪv dɪˈtɜːmɪnə]	Possessivbegleiter (besitzanzeigender Begleiter)	*my, your, his, her, its, our, your, their*
possessive form [pəˌzesɪv ˈfɔːm]	s-Genitiv	*Jo's brother; my friend's car*
possessive pronoun [pəˌzesɪv ˈprəʊnaʊn]	Possessivpronomen (besitzanzeigendes Pronomen)	*mine, yours, his, hers, ours, yours, theirs*
preposition [ˌprepəˈzɪʃn]	Präposition	*after, at, in, next to, over*
present participle [ˌpreznt ˈpɑːtɪsɪpl]	Partizip Präsens	*going, taking, watching*
present perfect [ˌpreznt ˈpɜːfɪkt]	*present perfect*	*I**'ve made** a cake for you.*
present perfect progressive [ˌpreznt ˌpɜːfɪkt prəˈgresɪv]	Verlaufsform des *present perfect*	*We**'ve been waiting** for over an hour.*
present progressive [ˌpreznt prəˈgresɪv]	Verlaufsform der Gegenwart	*Jack **is having** lunch.*
pronoun [ˈprəʊnaʊn]	Pronomen, Fürwort	
quantifier [ˈkwɒntɪfaɪə]	Mengenangabe	*much/many, some/any, …*
question [ˈkwestʃən]	Frage(satz)	
question tag [ˈkwestʃən tæg]	Frageanhängsel	*The song is great, **isn't it?***
question word	Fragewort	*who, what, why, how*
reflexive pronoun [rɪˌfleksɪv ˈprəʊnaʊn]	Reflexivpronomen	*myself, herself, ourselves, …*
regular verb [ˌregjələ ˈvɜːb]	regelmäßiges Verb	*(to) help – helped – helped*
relative clause [ˌrelətɪv ˈklɔːz]	Relativsatz	*The boy **who lives here** …*
relative pronoun [ˌrelətɪv ˈprəʊnaʊn]	Relativpronomen	*who, which, that, whose*
reported speech [rɪˌpɔːtɪd ˈspiːtʃ]	indirekte Rede	*He said his name was Paul.*
request [rɪˈkwest]	Bitte	*Could you close the door, please?*
s-**genitive** [ˈes ˌdʒenətɪv]	s-Genitiv	*Jo's brother; my friend's car*
short answer [ˌʃɔːt_ˈɑːnsə]	Kurzantwort	*Yes, I am. / No, he doesn't.*
simple past [ˌsɪmpl ˈpɑːst]	einfache Form der Vergangenheit	*Yesterday Dan **helped** Jo.*
simple present [ˌsɪmpl ˈpreznt]	einfache Form der Gegenwart	*I often **go** to school by bus.*

singular [ˈsɪŋgjələ]	Singular, Einzahl	
statement [ˈsteɪtmənt]	Aussage(satz)	*I like pop. / I don't like jazz.*
subject [ˈsʌbdʒɪkt]	Subjekt	***Jo** is writing a letter.*
subject form	Subjektform (der Personalpronomen)	*I, you, he, she, it, we, they*
subject question	Subjektfrage, Frage nach dem Subjekt	*Who likes bananas?*
subordinate clause [səˈbɔːdɪnət ˈklɔːz]	Nebensatz	***If I see Jack**, I'll tell him.*
subordinating conjunction	unterordnende Konjunktion,	*after, because, if, that, till,*
[səˌbɔːdɪneɪtɪŋ kənˈdʒʌŋkʃn]	subordinierende Konjunktion	*when*
uncountable noun [ʌnˈkaʊntəbl]	nicht zählbares Nomen	*bread, tea, money, time*
verb [vɜːb]	Verb	▶ *full verb, main verb*
verb [vɜːb] (= verb phrase)	Prädikat	*Reading **can be** fun.*
***will**-future* [ˈwɪl fjuːtʃə]	Futur mit *will*	*My sister **will be** 16 soon.*
word class [ˈwɜːd klɑːs]	Wortart	
(= part of speech)		
word order [ˈwɜːd ˌɔːdə]	Wortstellung	
yes/no question	Entscheidungsfrage	*Are you 13? Do you like judo?*

Lösungen

p. 8

1 **A** Who met Latisha at the festival?
  B Who did Katrina meet at the festival?
2 **A** Who wants to keep in touch with Asif?
  B Who does Robert want to keep in touch with?
3 **A** Who takes Katrina to the ferry every morning?
  B Who does Mrs McFadden take to the ferry every morning?

p. 9

1 Have you got my ruler? I **gave it to you** yesterday.
2 Didn't Mum say she wanted to **make me a cake**? Where is it? – No, no. Mum said she wanted **to make a cake for Dad**, not for you!
3 Could you **explain the problem to the team**, please?

p. 10

1 They **soon** found out why Jack had shouted **angrily**.
2 '**Perhaps** we can see the village from this tree,' he said and climbed it **carefully**.
3 I'm **often** nervous before a test. But I **usually** do **quite** well in the end.
4 I've **always** wanted to have a picnic **in Central Park on a warm summer evening**.

p. 14

1 My sister **usually has** milk for breakfast, but this morning she's **drinking** tea.
2 At the weekend we **often go** to Camden Lock Market with our friends.

3 Normally I **get up** at seven o'clock, but this week I'**m getting up** later because there's no school.
4 We **usually play** tennis at weekends, but this weekend we'**re visiting** friends in Bath.
5 'I can't talk to you right now. I'**m just washing** my hair.'

p. 18 a) When the earthquake started, …
1 Mrs Brown **was making** tea.
2 Mrs Brown **ran** out of the house.
When the lion escaped, …
3 John Webster **was having** a sandwich.
4 John Webster **had** a heart attack.

p. 18 b) Helen didn't go to the cinema because …
1 she **had left** her purse at home.
2 the queue **was** too long.
Jacob bought lots of apples because …
3 they **were** very cheap.
4 his mum **had asked** him to get some fruit.

p. 18 c) 1 But we'**ve already cycled** 20 km! – Come on. Yesterday we **cycled** 50 km without stopping.
2 But we'**ve seen** it! We **went** to see it last Friday.

p. 26 1 Grandma **will be** 80 next week. We'**re going to have** a big party for her.
2 Have you got any plans for this summer? – Yes, we'**re going to fly** to California.

3 Do you like your new flat? – Well, it's too small, really. We**'re going to move** out again. We've already started looking..

4 Are you free next Friday?
– No, I**'m meeting** Joanna.

5 Don't forget to take some warm clothes. It**'ll be** cold in Canada at this time of the year.

p. 31 a) 1 Our DVD player didn't work any more, so we **had to** buy a new one.

2 Do you think we**'ll be allowed to** use a dictionary in our English test tomorrow?

3 There was snow and ice on the road, but the driver **was able to** stop the car.

4 Little Jenny fell into the swimming pool. Luckily, she **was able to** pull herself out.

5 I'm sorry, I**'ll have to** go in a couple of minutes. I've got an appointment ...

6 I **wasn't allowed to** take my pocket knife on my flight to New York last week.

p. 31 b) 1 You **needn't** tell Dad about the trip. He already knows.

2 You **mustn't** tell Mum about the trip. It's a surprise.

p. 33 1 Manchester United's stadium **is called** 'Old Trafford'. It **was built** in 1909.

2 Maps and guide books **can be bought** at the visitor centre.

3 The new motorway **will be opened** by the Queen next Saturday.

4 Hundreds of concert tickets **have already been sold**.

5 Butter **should be kept** in the fridge.

6 In 1906, more than 2000 people **were killed** in an earthquake in California.

7 Fires that broke out after the earthquake **could not be put out** for days.

p. 34 1 My grandparents **were sent** a very funny postcard.

2 On my first day at school I **was shown** all the classrooms.

3 I was shocked when I **was told** the news.

4 You **will be given** a few minutes to read the questions before the test begins.

5 You won't believe it! I**'ve been offered** a job at the local gym.

p. 35 **1D**, **2A**, **3F**, **4B**, **5E**, **6C**

p. 37 a) 1 The teacher **told/wanted Jaden to clean** the board.

2 The policeman **wanted/told me to wait** outside.

3 We all **expected her to win** the competition.

4 Dad **would like us to tidy up** our rooms.

p. 37 b) 1 Can you tell me **how to get** to the cathedral?

2 I wasn't sure **who to believe**, my brother or my sister.

3 Computer games are OK if you know **when to stop**.

4 I was so embarrassed I didn't know **what to say**.

p. 39 1 We're planning **to spend** our holidays in Cornwall. You'll enjoy **surfing** the waves.

2 Mum and Dad have decided against **going** abroad this year.

3 I thought we had decided **to fly** to Spain? I've been looking forward to **lying** on the beach all day.

4 Have you finished **revising** your essay?

p. 40 1 Why is wine from Australia often cheaper than wine **produced** in Europe?

2 On the train we met some American students **travelling** through Europe.

3 My brother has got a job with a company **designing** computer games.

4 They've published a dictionary specially **designed** for students.

5 Cricket is a game **played** in many English-speaking countries.

p. 43 a) 1 The international news **is** at eight o'clock.

2 The police **were** waiting round the corner, with an ambulance behind **them**.

3 The black trousers **are** too tight, but the red jeans **look** good on you.

4 I have to wear **glasses** when I'm driving, but I don't need **them** to read.

5 The new equipment for the camera club **has** arrived. **It was** quite expensive, so please be careful.

p. 43 b) 1/2 pound of butter, 2 packets of coffee, 1 kilo of sugar, 2 bottles of milk, 1 piece of cheese

p. 47 **1B/B**, **2A**, **3C**, **4A**, **5C**, **6A/B**

p. 48 1 We don't get **much** snow where we live.

2 I don't drink **much** coffee. Just one cup in the morning.

3 **Few** people like his books because they're so difficult to read.

4 I can give you **some** money if you need it.

5 There are **a few** apples left in the bowl.

p. 51 1 We're going to meet in the park after school.

2 He hurt **himself** and had to sit down for a moment.

3 We talked to **each other** on the phone yesterday.

4 People who talk to **themselves** are a bit scary, I think.

5 Come on, we have to hurry or we'll be late. – Relax! We've got plenty of time!

6 I don't need your help. I can help **myself**.

p. 54 1 I picked up the little boy **carefully**. He smiled at me **happily**.

2 You look **tired**. Didn't you sleep **well**?

3 The exercise seemed **difficult** at first, but we were able to do it **easily** in the end.

4 I think dog food smells **awful**. I'm sure it tastes **horrible** too.

5 If you ask **nicely**, people will **usually** help you.

6 Although he tried to speak **slowly**, his voice didn't sound very **clear**.

7 She felt **great**. She was sure she had done **well** in the test.

p. 58/1 **1A**, **2B**, **3B**, **4B**, **5A**, **6A**

p. 58/2 1 If the shops hadn't been closed, we could have gone shopping.

2 If Claire had turned off her computer, it wouldn't have been on all night.

3 If I hadn't turned on the radio, I wouldn't have found out about the murders.

4 If he had locked his car, Mr Johnson's car radio wouldn't have been stolen.

5 If the weather had been good enough, we could have gone swimming.

p. 60 a) 1 There are a couple of things on the kitchen table that I need for the salad.

2 The woman who was taken to hospital last night is still unconscious.

3 The girl who saved a little boy from drowning got a medal.

4 I lost the book that John lent me.

p. 60 b) 1 **D** 15-year-old Stevie won the 100 metres, which surprised everybody.

2 **C** She called him silly and stupid, which was really rude of her.

3 **B** Dad has given up smoking, which will save him a lot of money.

4 **A** We're moving to Leeds in the summer, which means I'll have to change school.

p. 61 1 Have you kept in touch with that girl you met in Spain?

3 I've found the CD you've been looking for.

4 The hotel we stayed at was really nice, but quite expensive too.

5 Where's that book John sent from England?

p. 63 1 Colin told me that Chris Martin from *Coldplay* was his favourite singer.

2 Julie said that *Coldplay* were giving a free open-air concert in June.

3 Emily said that she had never been to an open-air concert.

4 Mark said he didn't like open-air concerts.

5 Colin said he thought they were great fun.

p. 64 a) 1 A girl asked me if I could look after her surfboard for a while.

2 A little boy wondered if he needed a ticket for his teddy bear.

3 A woman wanted to know/asked me where the nearest internet café was.

p. 64 b) 1 Can you tell me where I can park my car?

2 Excuse me, I'd like to know how long it takes to get to Bath.

3 Do you know when the post office opens?

p. 65 1 Mrs Waller told us to be quiet.

2 She asked us to listen.

3 She told Tim and Dan not to argue.

4 She asked Sue and Lucy to go and get the head teacher.

In diesem Teil des Heftes – dem **Skills**-Teil – sind
wichtige **Lern- und Arbeitstechniken** zusammengestellt.

Die Beispiele und Tipps helfen dir

– beim **Erlernen von Methoden**,

– bei der Arbeit mit **Hör- und Lesetexten**,

– beim **Sprechen und Schreiben**,

– bei der **Mediation (Sprachmittlung)**,

– bei der **Vorbereitung auf Tests und Prüfungen**.

3: 2 / 4: 6   Die Ziffern bei den Überschriften geben an,
wo das Thema in den Bänden 3 und 4 von
English G 21, Ausgabe A, behandelt wird
(hier: Band 3, Unit 2, und Band 4, Unit 6).

*Meist findest du am Ende der Abschnitte eine
kleine Aufgabe, mit der du überprüfen kannst,
ob du die Technik richtig anwenden kannst.
Auf den Seiten 92–94 kannst du überprüfen,
ob du die Aufgaben richtig gelöst hast.*

Inhalt

Skills

Study and language skills

1 Working with dictionaries (Mit Wörterbüchern arbeiten) 3:1 / 3:2 / 4:6

Wann kann mir ein zweisprachiges Wörterbuch helfen?

Du verstehst einen Text nicht, weil er zu viele Wörter enthält, die dir unbekannt sind, und die Worterschließungstechniken (▶ *Working out the meaning of words*, p. 82) helfen dir nicht weiter?
Du sollst einen Text auf Englisch schreiben, und dir fehlt das eine oder andere Wort, um deine Ideen auszudrücken?
In diesen Fällen hilft dir ein zweisprachiges Wörterbuch.

1. Die **Leitwörter** *(running heads)* am Kopf der Seiten helfen dir, den gesuchten Wörterbucheintrag schneller zu finden. Auf der linken Seite oben steht der erste Eintrag, auf der rechten Seite oben der letzte Eintrag der jeweiligen Doppelseite.

2. Die blau gedruckten **Stichwörter** *(headwords)* sind alphabetisch angeordnet: **a** vor **b**, **ap** vor **aq**, **apr** vor **apt** usw.

3. Die **Lautschrift** gibt an, wie das Wort ausgesprochen und betont wird.

4. Die **Ziffern 1., 2.** usw. zeigen, dass ein Stichwort mehrere ganz verschiedene Bedeutungen hat (und manchmal auch verschiedenen Wortarten angehört).

5. *Kursiv* **gedruckte Hinweise** helfen dir, die passende Bedeutung zu finden. Beachte auch die Angaben zur Wortart, die Angaben zur Verwendung sowie die Hinweise auf unregelmäßige Verbformen, auf besondere Steigerungsformen und Ähnliches im englisch-deutschen Teil.

6. In manchen Wörterbüchern ersetzt eine **Tilde (~)** das Stichwort in Beispielsätzen und Redewendungen.

7. In vielen Wörterbüchern gibt es zu kniffligen Wörtern zusätzliche **Info-Kästchen**, in denen du weitere nützliche Hilfen und Hinweise findest.

---

award

avert [əˈvɜːt] *Krise o. Ä.* abwenden; **~ one's eyes** den Blick abwenden; **~ an accident** einen Unfall verhindern
aviation [ˌeɪviˈeɪʃn] Luftfahrt
avid [ˈævɪd] begeistert
avoid [əˈvɔɪd] vermeiden; *Ort* meiden; *Hindernis* ausweichen; **~ sb.** jm. aus dem Weg gehen; **~ doing sth.** es vermeiden, etwas zu tun
avoidable [əˈvɔɪdəbl] vermeidbar
await [əˈweɪt] *förmlich* erwarten
awake [əˈweɪk] wach; *it's keeping me ~* das hält mich wach; **wide ~** hellwach
award [əˈwɔːd] **1** *Nomen* Preis, Auszeichnung **2** *Verb mit Obj;* Auszeichnung, Preis verleihen; *she was awarded the Nobel Prize* ihr wurde der Nobelpreis verliehen; *be awarded damages* Schadenersatz zugesprochen bekommen

---

dann

dann then; *wenn sie es nicht schafft, wer ~?* if she can't do it, then who can?; **~ und wann** (every) now and then; **bis ~!** see you later!; **~ eben nicht** well, don't then, suit yourself
daran *räumlich* on it; *etwas befestigen* to it; *denken* about it; *sterben* of it; *glauben* in it; *leiden* from it; *arbeiten* on it; **~ liegt es (, dass …)** that's why (...)
darangehen get* down to it; **~, etwas zu tun** get* down to doing sth.
darauf *räumlich* on it; *zeitlich* after that; *hören, antworten, trinken* to it; *stolz* of it; *warten* for it; **bald ~** soon after; **am Tag ~** the day after, the next day; **~ kommt es an** that's what matters
daraufhin *danach* after that; *als Folge* as a result; *etwas ~ prüfen, ob …* test sth. to see if ...

Ja, danke. – Nein, danke.

Wenn man ein **Angebot annehmen** möchte, sagt man meist **Yes, please**:

– Möchtest du etwas zu trinken?	– Would you like something to drink?
– **Ja gern, danke.**	– Yes, please.

Wenn man ein **Angebot ablehnen** möchte, sagt man **No, thank you** oder **No, thanks**:

– Möchtest du etwas zu trinken?	– Would you like something to drink?
– **Nein, danke. / Danke, nein.**	– No, thank you. / No, thanks.

⚠ Im Deutschen kann man ein Angebot durch ein einfaches **Danke** (begleitet von

---

Tipp

Lies den **gesamten Wörterbucheintrag**, bevor du dich für eine Übersetzung entscheidest. Nimm nicht einfach die erste Übersetzung, die dir angeboten wird.

Kannst du die folgenden Sätze mithilfe der Wörterbuchauszüge übersetzen?

a) Who was **awarded** the first prize?
b) They couldn't **avert** the crisis.
c) The noise kept him **awake** all night.
d) Luckily the driver was able to **avoid** the dog.

e) Nicht schon wieder Pizza! – Was **dann**?
f) Wir arbeiten **daran**.
g) Du solltest nicht **darauf** warten.
h) Ich bin stolz **darauf**.

Wann kann mir ein einsprachiges Wörterbuch helfen?

Wenn du englische Texte liest oder einen englischen Text schreibst, kannst du auch ein einsprachiges englisches Wörterbuch *(an English–English dictionary)* verwenden. Dort findest du mehr über die korrekte Verwendung englischer Wörter und Wendungen heraus als in einem zweisprachigen Wörterbuch:

1. Einsprachige Wörterbücher erklären **die Bedeutung eines englischen Wortes auf Englisch**. Da viele Wörter mehrere Bedeutungen haben, solltest du alle Einträge und Beispielsätze genau lesen und mit deinem englischen Text vergleichen, um die passende Bedeutung herauszufinden.

2. Wenn du selbst einen englischen Text schreibst, ist es wichtig zu wissen, wie du „dein Wort" richtig im Zusammenhang verwendest. Ein einsprachiges Wörterbuch gibt Antworten auf Fragen wie **„Mit welchen Verben steht dieses Nomen?"** oder **„Welche Präposition muss ich mit diesem Wort verwenden?"**

3. Wenn du die **englische Entsprechung eines deutschen Wortes** suchst und kein deutsch-englisches Wörterbuch benutzen kannst oder darfst, dann hilft dir ein einsprachiges Wörterbuch nur, wenn du Teile des Wortes oder des Ausdrucks schon kennst oder eine vage Ahnung hast, wie die englische Entsprechung heißen könnte. Angenommen, du suchst die Entsprechung des Wortes „todernst". Kennst du einen der beiden Teile des Wortes? Was heißt „Tod" oder „tot"? Was heißt „ernst"? (Findest du die Lösung im Wörterbuchauszug rechts?)

> **deadly** ['dedli] *adj*
> **1** *able or likely to kill people* {= lethal}: This is no longer a deadly disease.
> **deadly to** The HSN virus is deadly to chickens.
> **a deadly weapon** The new generation of biological weapons is more deadly than ever.
> **2** *(only before noun)* {= complete}: **deadly silence** There was deadly silence after his speech.
> **a deadly secret** Don't tell anyone – this is a deadly secret.
> **in deadly earnest** *completely serious:* Don't you laugh – I am in deadly earnest!
> **3** *(informal) very boring:* Many TV programmes are pretty deadly!
> **4** *always able to achieve something:* The new Chelsea striker is said to be a deadly goal scorer.

1 Beantworte diese Fragen mithilfe eines einsprachigen Wörterbuchs.

a) Was ist der Unterschied zwischen *critic* und *criticism*?
b) Wo sagt man *lift*, wo sagt man *elevator*?
c) Wie spricht man *sew* („nähen") aus, und wie lauten die drei Formen?

2 Wie drückt man das auf Englisch aus? Und wo würdest du nachschlagen?

a) etwas gut können
b) jm. einen Streich spielen
c) eine Erfahrung machen
d) bei jm. beliebt sein

2 Describing and analysing pictures (Bilder beschreiben und analysieren)

Beschreibung: Wo ist was? / Wer tut was?

– Um zu sagen, wo genau etwas abgebildet ist, verwende:
   at the top/bottom · in the foreground/background · in the middle · on the left/right above · behind · between · in front of · next to · under
   Du kannst diese phrases auch kombinieren:
   at the bottom on the left · in the background on the right

– Um zu beschreiben, was die Personen auf dem Bild tun, verwende das ***present progressive***:
   *The girls **are looking at** a music magazine. ...*

Analyse/Interpretation: Wer fühlt was?

Wenn du dich in die abgebildeten Personen hineinversetzen und beschreiben sollst, was sie fühlen oder denken, kannst du diese Ausdrücke verwenden:
Maybe the boy in the photo feels ... / is thinking about ... · I think he might want to ... · To me the girls look as if they ...

Sieh dir das Foto an. Beschreibe und analysiere es. Wie, glaubst du, fühlen sich die Mädchen? Und der Junge? Es hilft, wenn du dir vorher Notizen machst. (▶ Taking notes, p. 81) Gib die Bildbeschreibung deinem Lehrer/ deiner Lehrerin und bitte ihn/sie, deinen Text zu korrigieren.

3 Outlines (Gliederungen)   4: 3

Stell dir vor, du sollst zu einem komplexen Thema einen Text schreiben oder eine Präsentation vorbereiten. Bevor du mit dem Sammeln von Informationen und Unterlagen beginnst (► *Research*, pp. 77–78), solltest du eine **Gliederung** *(outline)* erstellen. Das Erstellen einer Gliederung hilft dir, deine Ideen zu organisieren und deinen Text vorzustrukturieren. Mithilfe einer guten Gliederung kannst du gezielter nach Informationen suchen.

Gliederungen werden in **Stichpunkten** oder kurzen Sätzen verfasst. Schreibe zunächst die **wichtigsten Aspekte** auf. Bestimme dann **Unterthemen** und überlege dir, welche Beispiele und Erläuterungen du geben möchtest. Am Rand des Blattes kannst du vermerken, welche **Bilder, Zitate, Statistiken** usw. du einsetzen möchtest.

Die Gliederung dient dir als **Ausgangspunkt** für deinen Text bzw. deine Präsentation. Und sie gibt deinen Lesern oder Zuhörern einen **Überblick über dein Thema**, wenn du deinen Text bzw. deine Präsentation mit der Gliederung beginnen lässt (bei einem mündlichen Vortrag kannst du sie z.B. mithilfe einer Folie oder eines Beamers an die Wand projizieren).

The Civil Rights Movement

<u>*OUTLINE*</u>

I. History
  A. Slaves and plantations   *pictures*
  B. The Civil War   *figures, names*

II. The Civil Rights Movement
  A. Martin Luther King   *photo, DVD*
    1. Excerpt from speech   *CD, handout*
    2. Short film sequence   *DVD*
  B. The Montgomery Bus Boycott
  C. The Little Rock Nine   *photo, DVD*

III. Famous African Americans today

Dein Thema für eine Präsentation lautet **Schools in the USA**. *Wie würdest du diese Stichpunkte gliedern?*

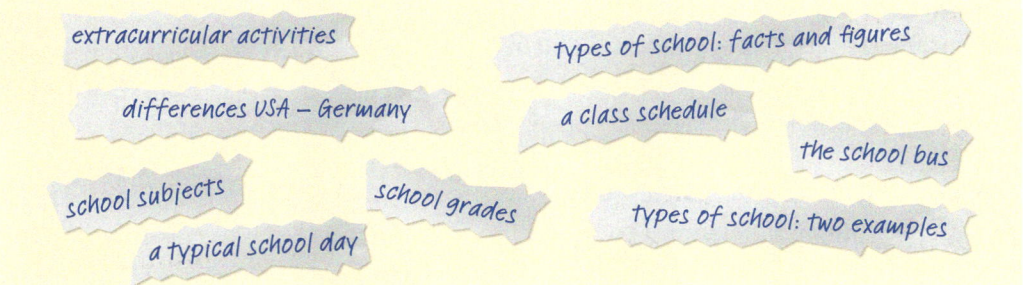

extracurricular activities

differences USA – Germany

school subjects

school grades

a typical school day

types of school: facts and figures

a class schedule

the school bus

types of school: two examples

---

4 Research (Recherche)   3: 5 / 4: 5

Material sammeln

Wenn du zu einem Thema etwas schreiben oder einen Vortrag halten sollst, dann brauchst du **informatives Material**.

Du solltest immer **mehrere, möglichst englischsprachige Quellen** verwenden. Sammle alles in einem **Ordner** und **sortiere** dabei das Material gemäß deiner Gliederung (► *Outlines*, p. 77).

Achte immer darauf, ob es sich um **sachliche Informationen**, also Tatsachen, oder um **persönliche Meinungen** handelt.

King, Martin Luther

(Fortsetzung ► p. 78)

Recherchieren im Internet

Das Hauptproblem bei der Recherche im Internet ist, dass du oft **zu viele Informationen** findest.
Diese Tipps sollen dir dabei helfen, nicht im *world wide web* verloren zu gehen.

– Notiere zuerst die wichtigsten Stichwörter – die **Schlüsselwörter** *(key words)* – für dein Thema, also z.B.
  African Americans, history, USA, Civil Rights Movement, ...
– Überlege, welches Stichwort oder welche Kombination von Stichwörtern gute Ergebnisse liefern könnte:
  „African Americans" history oder **African+Americans+history** oder **...**
  (Die Anführungsstriche bei „African Americans" sorgen dafür, dass nur solche Websites angezeigt werden,
  auf denen diese beiden Wörter tatsächlich direkt nebeneinander vorkommen.)
– **Suchmaschinen** wie *Google* oder *Yahoo* helfen dir, mithilfe deiner Schlüsselwörter Websites zu deinem Thema zu
  finden. Wenn die angezeigten Websites dir nicht helfen oder du zu viele Websites angezeigt bekommst, versuch es
  noch einmal, indem du deine Schlüsselwörter präzisierst oder ergänzt.
– Wenn du dir zunächst einen Überblick verschaffen willst, kannst du auch ein **Nachschlagewerk im Internet**
  anklicken: www.infoplease.com oder www.en.wikipedia.org
  Manchmal gibt es dort auch Links, die dir weiterhelfen können.

Wichtiges herausschreiben (exzerpieren)

Sichte das Material und entscheide, welche Informationen du tatsächlich verwenden möchtest.
– **Informationen aus Büchern und Zeitschriften** schreibst du heraus, oder du machst Fotokopien. Auf den Kopien
  kannst du wichtige Passagen markieren (▶ *Marking up texts*, p. 81). Eigene Gedanken fügst du in Stichpunkten
  hinzu. Vergiss die **Quellenangabe** nicht!
– **Internet-Materialien** sammelst du zunächst in elektronischen Ordnern auf deinem Rechner. Dann überträgst du
  die wichtigsten Informationen mit den Befehlen „Kopieren" und „Einfügen" in ein neues Dokument, wo du sie
  dann bearbeiten kannst (also kürzen, ergänzen, umschreiben usw.). Vergiss auch hier die **Quellenangabe** nicht!

Umschreiben – zitieren – Quellen angeben

Nun kannst du darangehen, deinen Text oder deine Präsentation auszuformulieren. Dabei solltest du nicht einfach
aus deinen Quellen abschreiben. Verwende **eigene Formulierungen**!

Wenn du deine Argumentation mit Expertenaussagen unterstützen oder deinen Text mit einem Auszug aus einem
Buch, einem Interview o.Ä. interessanter und abwechslungsreicher gestalten möchtest, markiere solche **Zitate** durch
Anführungszeichen und gib **Autor und Quelle** einschließlich Seitenzahl an (bei Internetquellen die Webadresse und
das Datum des Aufrufs). Das gilt auch dann, wenn du
eine fremde Aussage mit eigenen Worten umschreibst.
Auch bei Abbildungen musst du die Quelle angeben.
Bei einer mündlichen Präsentation solltest du Zitate
ankündigen. Achte auf logische Übergänge zu deinen
eigenen Argumenten.

Und denk daran: Lange Zitate können auch ermüdend
wirken und vielleicht den Eindruck erwecken, dass du
selbst nur wenig zu sagen hast.

> **Tipp**
>
> – Verwende immer mehrere Quellen!
> – Nicht alles, was im Internet steht, ist richtig!
>   Schau immer mehr als eine Website an, um
>   sicherzugehen, dass die Informationen stimmen.
> – Bei englischen Quellen brauchst du nicht jedes
>   Detail zu verstehen. Konzentriere dich auf das
>   Wesentliche. (▶ *Skimming and scanning*, p. 82)

Welche Ratschläge sind schlecht? Verbessere sie.

a) Kürze Zitate nie.
b) Drucke immer alle Internetseiten sofort aus.
c) Verwende Anführungsstriche, wenn deine
   Stichwörter als zusammenhängender Such-
   begriff verstanden werden sollen.
d) Gib nur bei Texten die Quelle an.

e) Notiere erst die wichtigsten Stichwörter.
f) Ordne dein Material mithilfe deiner Stichpunkte bzw. deiner Gliederung.
g) Zitiere deine Quellen immer wörtlich.
h) Verwende immer mehrere Quellen.

5 Presentations (Präsentationen)

■ Vorbereitung.

– Ordne und notiere deine Gedanken (in Stichworten),
z.B. auf nummerierten Karteikarten oder als Mindmap.
Eine Gliederung hilft dir, deine Ideen zu organisieren (▶ *Outlines*, p. 77).
– Bereite ein Poster, eine Folie oder ein Handout vor (▶ *Handouts*, p. 79).
(Alternativ kannst du auch mit Computer und Beamer arbeiten.)
Schreib groß und für alle gut lesbar.
– Übe deine Präsentation zu Hause vor einem Spiegel.
Sprich laut, deutlich und langsam. Mach Pausen.
Reicht die Zeit?

■ Durchführung

– Bevor du beginnst, bereite deine Medien vor und sortiere deine Vortragskarten.
Überprüfe, ob die Technik im Vortragsraum funktioniert.
– Warte, bis es ruhig ist. Schau die Zuhörer an.
– Erkläre zu Anfang, worüber du sprechen wirst. Deine Gliederung – auf dem Handout,
als Folie oder an der Tafel – kann deinen Zuhörern helfen, deiner Präsentation zu folgen.
– Lies nicht von deinen Karten ab, sondern sprich möglichst frei.
– Schreibe unbekannten Wortschatz und Eigennamen an die Tafel.

■ Schluss

– Sag, dass du fertig bist.
– Frag die Zuhörenden, ob sie Fragen haben.
– Bedanke dich fürs Zuhören.

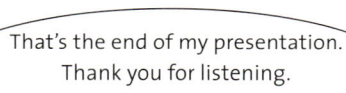

That's the end of my presentation.
Thank you for listening.
Have you got any questions?

6 Handouts (Handzettel)   4:2

Oje!?!?

Ein **Handout** enthält die wichtigsten Aussagen einer Präsentation.
Manchmal bietet es auch zusätzliche Informationen, z.B. Statistiken,
Zitate, Quellenangaben oder Illustrationen.

Ein Handout kannst du **vor**, **während** oder **nach** deiner Präsentation austeilen:
– vor oder während der Präsentation, damit die Zuhörenden die Gliederung
deines Vortrags nachvollziehen und ihm besser folgen können;
– nach der Präsentation, damit die Zuhörenden später noch einmal
nachlesen und sich besser an die Präsentation erinnern können.

Strukturiere dein Handout klar und übersichtlich, z.B. durch Überschriften,
durch Beispiele, durch tabellarische oder grafische Übersichten.
Dein Handout sollte auch deinen Namen und das Datum der Präsentation
enthalten.

Du kannst **in ganzen Sätzen** schreiben, z.B. wenn du eine
Zusammenfassung geben willst, oder in **Stichpunkten**.

Wenn du **Abbildungen** verwendest, gib ihnen
eine Bildunterschrift und vergiss nicht die
Quellenangabe. Mit **Symbolen** kannst du dein
Handout übersichtlicher gestalten und wesentliche Informationen hervorheben.

Lass ausreichend **Platz für Notizen** der Zuhörer,
z.B. durch einen breiten Rand.

*Stell dir vor, du sollst für jüngere
Schüler/innen eine kleine Präsentation
halten zum Thema*

„Die wichtigsten Regeln für eine
gute Präsentation".

*Entwirf ein Handout, das du nach
deinem Vortrag austeilen kannst.
Wie würde dein Handout aussehen?*

Listening and reading skills

7 Listening (Hörverstehen)   3:1

■ **Vor dem Hören**
- Frag dich, was du schon über das Thema weißt.
- Nutze Überschriften und Bilder, um eine Vorstellung zu bekommen, um was es in deinem Hörtext gehen könnte.
- Lies dir die Aufgaben zu deinem Hörtext genau durch. Überlege, auf welche Informationen du dich konzentrieren musst.
- Finde heraus, ob du den Hörtext einmal oder zweimal hören wirst.
- Bereite dich darauf vor, Notizen zu machen. Je nach Aufgabe kannst du z.B. eine Tabelle oder Liste anlegen (▶ *Taking notes*, p. 81).

■ **Während des Hörens**

1. *Listening for gist:*
Wenn du den Text zweimal hören kannst, dann konzentriere dich beim ersten Hören auf **allgemeine Informationen**, z.B. die Personen (unterschiedliche Stimmen), das Thema, die Umgebung (Geräusche), die Atmosphäre (die Sprechweise der Personen).

2. *Listening for detail:*
- Mach dir noch einmal bewusst, welche **Einzelheiten** du heraushören sollst bzw. willst. Lass dich nicht von anderen Einzelheiten oder Geräuschen ablenken.
- Gerate nicht in Panik, wenn du meinst, du hättest etwas Wichtiges verpasst. Konzentriere dich auf die nächste wichtige Information.
- Halte deine Notizen kurz (**Stichworte, Abkürzungen, Symbole, ...**).
- Manche **Signalwörter** machen es dir leichter, den Hörtext zu verstehen:
  and, another, too (Aufzählung)
  although, but (Gegensatz)
  because, so, so that (Grund, Folge)
  better/older/... than, as ... as, more ..., most ... (Vergleich)
  before, after, then, next, later, when, at last, at the same time (Reihenfolge).
- Auch die **Stimme**, der **Akzent** und der **Tonfall** des Sprechers/der Sprecherin können dir wichtige Informationen geben (Herkunft, Gefühle, Absichten, ...).

> **!** Beim Hören von **Telefonansagen** fehlt dir der Blickkontakt. Bereite dich daher besonders gut vor:
> - Überlege vorher genau, welche Informationen du heraushören willst.
> - Horche auf die entsprechenden Schlüsselwörter.
> - Wenn möglich, mache Notizen während des Hörens.
> Die meisten Telefonansagen kann man mehrmals anhören.
> Also keine Panik!

■ **Nach dem Hören**
- Vervollständige deine Notizen sofort.
- Wenn du den Text ein weiteres Mal hören kannst, konzentriere dich auf das, was du vorher nicht genau verstanden hast.

> **Tipp**
>
> Du kannst viele DVDs auch mit englischem Ton ansehen.Nutze diese Gelegenheit so oft wie möglich. (Ob du den englischen Ton besser verstehst, wenn du die deutschen Untertitel liest, musst du ausprobieren.)

8 Marking up texts (Texte markieren)

Du bereitest eine Präsentation oder einen Bericht vor und hast einen Text mit vielen Fakten vor dir liegen. Dann wird es dir helfen, die für deine Aufgabenstellung **wichtigen Informationen** im Text zu markieren.

Markiere nicht zu viel – nicht jeder Satz enthält Informationen, die für dich wichtig sind. Und oft reicht es aus, nur ein oder zwei Wörter in einem Satz zu markieren.

> **!** Markiere nur **auf Fotokopien** oder **in deinen eigenen Büchern.**

Wichtige Wörter kannst du

– einkreisen – farbig <u>unterstreichen</u> – mit Textmarker hervorheben.

9 Taking notes (Notizen machen)

Wenn du beim Lesen oder Zuhören Notizen machst, kannst du dich später besser erinnern – z.B. wenn du etwas vortragen willst, etwas nacherzählen sollst oder einen Bericht schreiben musst.

Achte auf die **Schlüsselwörter** *(key words)* in Texten oder Gesprächen – nur <u>die</u> solltest du notieren. Meist sind das Substantive und Verben, manchmal auch Adjektive oder Zahlen.

Je nachdem, mit welchem Ziel bzw. mit welcher Aufgabenstellung du einen Text liest oder hörst, kannst du deine Notizen vorbereiten, indem du beispielsweise vor dem Lesen/Hören eine **Tabelle** oder **Liste** anlegst.

> **Tipp**
>
> Verwende **Ziffern, Symbole** und **Abkürzungen**, um Zeit zu sparen.

Jeder in der Klasse soll ein Buch vorstellen, welches er/sie gern lesen möchte. Du hast den Text rechts über Stephenie Meyers Buch Twilight *gefunden und möchtest ihn für eine kurze Präsentation aufbereiten.*

***Markiere** die Informationen, die für deine Vorstellung wichtig sind, und mach dir **Notizen**.*

Twilight is a love story about 17-year-old Bella and Edward, a boy with dreamy good looks who, Bella learns, is really a vampire. But this is no ordinary vampire story – it's a book in a class of its own which readers of all ages will definitely enjoy.

The story is told by Bella, and because she is the narrator we don't learn directly how the other characters feel or think. This increases the suspense. At first we know only a little about Edward and his family, but as the story develops we slowly get a bigger picture of these outsiders. Our appetite for more grows. What makes the story even more readable is that Bella is a very credible character, shy and without much self-confidence, but very likeable nevertheless.

Twilight is extremely well written, in language that is easy to understand. When you read about Forks, the town where the story is set, you feel as if you are there, walking through the permanent mist and rain.

A romance like this will move even the toughest of readers to tears. You won't put the book down until you have turned the very last page. Can the love between the two heroes survive? Will the two lovers themselves survive? Buy the book and find out.

10 Reading course – SUMMARY (Lesekurs – Zusammenfassung)

Working out the meaning of words

Das Nachschlagen unbekannter Wörter im Wörterbuch kostet Zeit und nimmt auf Dauer den Spaß am Lesen. Oft geht es auch ohne:

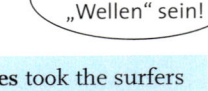

Waves müssen „Wellen" sein!

1. **Bilder** erklären und ergänzen oft die Aussagen im Text.

2. Oft hilft dir der **Textzusammenhang** *(context)*.

The **waves** took the surfers right onto the beach.

3. Zu manchen **englischen Wörtern** fallen dir vielleicht **Wörter aus anderen Sprachen** ein, die ähnlich geschrieben oder ausgesprochen werden.

excellent • colony • gallery • magical • nationality • reality • shock

4. Manchmal stecken in unbekannten Wörter **bekannte Teile**.

decision • energetic • indoors • owner • personality • sleeping bag • sporty

Skimming and scanning   3: 5 / 4: 2

■ *Skimming:* **Texte überfliegen**
Beim *Skimming* **überfliegst** du einen Text schnell, um dir einen Überblick zu verschaffen.
Du willst dabei herausfinden, ob der Text überhaupt für deine Zwecke und deine Aufgabenstellung geeignet ist.
Achte beim Überfliegen des Textes auf
– die **Überschrift**
– **Zwischenüberschriften** und **hervorgehobene** Wörter oder Sätze
– **Bilder** und **Bildunterschriften**
– den **ersten** und den **letzten Satz** eines jeden Absatzes
– **Grafiken, Statistiken** und die **Quelle** des Textes.

■ *Scanning:* **Texte nach bestimmten Informationen absuchen**
Beim *Scanning* suchst du nach **bestimmten Informationen** und **Details.**
Dabei suchst du den Text nach **Schlüsselwörtern** *(key words)* ab und liest dann nur an den Stellen weiter, wo du die Schlüsselwörter findest.
Wenn du deine Schlüsselwörter nicht entdeckst, versuche es noch einmal mit anderen, themenverwandten Wörtern – wenn du z.B. das Wort *meat* nicht finden konntest, versuche es mit *beef, pork* oder *chicken.*

Finding the main ideas of a text   4: 3

Zeitungsartikel, Berichte oder Kommentare verstehst du besser, wenn du die **wichtigsten Aussagen** erkennst und nachvollziehst, wie sie zusammenhängen.
Dabei hilft dir ein Blick auf die Struktur dieser Texte:

1. Jeder Text hat ein **Thema** mit mindestens einer **Hauptaussage**. Diese Hauptaussage findest du oft im **ersten Absatz**. Daher solltest du den ersten Absatz immer besonders gründlich lesen.

2. Die Hauptaussage wird in der Regel durch weitere wichtige Aussagen und Gedanken unterstützt. Diese weiteren wichtigen Ideen stehen oft am Beginn von neuen Absätzen.

3. **Beispiele** und **Begründungen** ergänzen die Aussagen des Textes.

Today, Canada is a truly multicultural place. The first Europeans who visited Canada were the Vikings, around the year 1000. Then, in 1497, a man called John Cabot left Bristol, crossed the Atlantic and landed on Canada's east coast.

In the 16th century the first French settlers in Canada lived near a mountain they called Mont Réal. Canada became a French colony, New France. But in 1763 France lost Canada to the British.

Most people in Canada are still of French or British descent, but people from many other parts of the world have also come to live there. Vancouver, for example, is sometimes called 'Hongcouver' or 'Vankong' because of all the Chinese immigrants. In Toronto, 40% of the people now belong to

Drawing conclusions   4: 4

Wenn du Fragen zu einem Text beantworten sollst oder bestimmte Informationen in einem Text suchst, kann es gut sein, dass du an mehreren Stellen schauen musst oder dass die Antwort nicht direkt im Text steht, sondern erschlossen werden muss. Dann ist sorgfältiges, schlussfolgerndes Lesen nötig:

1. Lies den Text genau. Welches sind seine **wesentlichen Aussagen**?
   (▶ *Finding the main ideas of a text*, p. 82)
   An welchen Stellen findest du die **Detailinformationen**, die du brauchst?
   (▶ *Scanning*, p. 82)
2. Führe die für dich wichtigen Informationen aus verschiedenen Textstellen zusammen, indem du sie im Text markierst (aber nur auf Kopien oder in eigenen Büchern!) und dann in Stichworten herausschreibst.
   (▶ *Marking up texts / Taking notes*, p. 81)
3. Manchmal steht die Antwort auf eine Frage <u>nicht direkt</u> im Text. Dann musst du **Schlussfolgerungen** ziehen aus all den Stellen im Text, die etwas mit deiner Frage zu tun haben.

1 *Wovon handelt der Text rechts?*

2 *Was sind für dich die wesentlichen Aussagen des Textes?*

3 *Welche Schlüsse kannst du aus dem Text über Kindheit* (childhood)*, Ausbildung, Zukunftschancen von Kindern wie J. ziehen?*

Text types: fiction and non-fiction   4: 5

Texte können entweder von einer Welt handeln, die vom Autor/von der Autorin erdacht wurde *(fictional texts)*, oder sich mit der realen Welt, mit Tatsachen auseinandersetzen *(non-fictional texts)*.

■ **Fiktionale Texte** sind z. B. **Kurzgeschichten** und **Romane**.
– Der Autor/Die Autorin wählt **Figuren *(characters)*** aus und erzählt von ihren Gefühlen und Handlungen und von deren Motiven und Hintergründen.
– Die **Handlungen** finden in einem oder mehreren **Handlungsrahmen** statt, z. B. an einem Ort, zu einer bestimmten Zeit, unter bestimmten Umständen *(setting)*.
– Die Ereignisse können aus verschiedenen **Perspektiven** erzählt werden *(point of view)*. Der Autor/Die Autorin wählt einen **Erzähler *(narrator)*** – das kann einer der Charaktere sein oder eine Person, die die Handlung von außen beobachtet.

■ **Nicht-fiktionale Texte** sind z. B. Zeitungsberichte, wissenschaftliche Artikel, Aufsätze oder Kommentare. Hier informiert der Autor/die Autorin über ein Thema der realen Welt (und nimmt manchmal auch Stellung dazu).

Es gibt auch Texte, die eine **Mischform** aus beiden Textarten sind.

Lies die beiden Texte rechts und beantworte die folgenden Fragen.

1 *Welche Figuren* (characters) *werden in den Texten erwähnt?*

2 *Was ist der Handlungsrahmen* (setting)?

3 *Aus welcher Perspektive* (point of view) *wird erzählt? Wer ist der Erzähler* (narrator)?

Every year, about 300,000 children between the ages of 6 and 14 move to northern Mexico with their parents to work in the fields.

J. is just ten years old, but he has been in these fields since he was seven. His working day begins long before the sun rises. He picks chili peppers eight hours a day and earns about seven US dollars.

When J. finishes working he will go to a school run by the company that employs him and his family. He will study for two to three hours and then return to camp to get some sleep before the next day begins.

When I came home from school on Friday afternoon, the German girl, Anna, was already there. She was another one of the exchange students who often stayed with us. It was really bad timing for me because I had a football match on Saturday. I said hello and tried to disappear into my room. 'I've got homework,' I told Anna and my mum. 'Latisha, we have a guest,' Mum answered.

On Friday morning the film crew and Katrina took the ferry to Hoy. They filmed Katrina as she stood at the front of the boat with the wind in her hair.
When they arrived in Lyness, Bill was talking to the ferry captain. The film crew and the passengers got off the boat, then Bill spoke to Katrina.
'OK, Katrina, back on the boat.'

Speaking and writing skills

11 Paraphrasing (Paraphrasieren)   3: 3

Paraphrasing bedeutet, etwas mit anderen Worten zu erklären, z.B. wenn dir ein bestimmtes Wort nicht einfällt oder wenn dein Gegenüber dich nicht verstanden hat (*(to) paraphrase* = „umschreiben, paraphrasieren").
Die Technik des Paraphrasierens ist besonders nützlich für die Mediation (▶ *Mediation*, p. 89).

– Du kannst Ausdrücke verwenden, die **dieselbe Bedeutung** haben (1). Oder du nennst das **Gegenteil** (2).

– Du kannst ein **allgemeineres Wort** oder einen **Überbegriff** verwenden und **weitere Eigenschaften** nennen (3, 4). Besonders gut funktioniert das mit **Relativsätzen** (5). (▶ *Relative clauses*, pp. 59–61)

(1) **'repeat'** means / is the same as / is another word for **'say again'**.
(2) **'dry'** is the opposite of **'wet'**.

(3) A **mug** is a kind of **big cup** for tea or coffee.
(4) A **ladle** is a large **spoon** / is a kind of large **spoon** – you use it to put soup onto a plate.
(5) A **recipe** is a **text** that tells you how to cook a dish.

Umschreibe die Wörter im Kästchen auf Englisch.
(Schlage danach die englische Entsprechung der deutschen Wörter in einem zweisprachigen Wörterbuch nach – oder online, z.B. bei **www.dict.cc***)*

a) Pfütze   d) a caravan
b) Balkon   e) a paddle
c) Spargel   f) cloudy

12 Brainstorming (Ideen sammeln)   3: 4

Bei vielen Aufgaben ist es nützlich, wenn du als Erstes möglichst viele Ideen zum Thema sammelst.

■ *Making a list:* Du kannst die Ideen so aufschreiben, wie sie dir einfallen – jede Idee kommt in eine neue Zeile. Erst in einem zweiten Schritt liest du alle Ideen durch und überlegst, welche für dein Thema wirklich sinnvoll sind. Dann nummerierst du die Ideen nach Nützlichkeit.

■ *Making a mind map:* Du kannst deine Ideen als Mindmap anordnen. Überlege, welche Oberbegriffe zu deinem Thema passen. Verwende unterschiedliche Farben für jeden Oberbegriff. Ergänze jede weitere Idee auf einem Nebenast. Notiere nur wichtige Schlüsselwörter – oder verwende Symbole und kleine Zeichnungen.

■ *The 5 Ws:* Schreib die fünf Fragewörter Who? What? When? Where? Why? in eine Tabelle. Dann notierst du deine Ideen zu jeder Frage in der Tabelle.

PARTY
buy food
buy drinks
talk to parents
invite friends
prepare room
buy decoration
make cake
look for good music
ask friends for help

1 Sieh dir die Party-Liste rechts an. Nummeriere die zu erledigenden Dinge so, dass eine für dich sinnvolle Reihenfolge entsteht. (Es gibt natürlich nicht nur eine „richtige" Möglichkeit.)

2 Kopiere die Tabelle und ergänze weitere Ideen für eine **Vampir-Geschichte**. (Schreib mithilfe der Tabelle eine Vampirgeschichte und bitte deine/n Lehrer/in, sie zu korrigieren.)

who?	what?	when?	where?	why?
a vampire a girl			in France in a castle	

13 Writing summaries (Zusammenfassungen schreiben) 4: 4

Wenn du einen Lese- oder Hörtext oder einen Filmausschnitt zusammenfassen möchtest, schreibst du eine **summary**. Dabei gehst du folgendermaßen vor:

1. Lies dir den Text noch mindestens einmal genau durch (bzw. hör ihn dir ein weiteres Mal an oder sieh dir den Filmausschnitt noch einmal an). Du kannst am Rand des Textes kurze Anmerkungen notieren. Auch bei Hörtexten und Filmausschnitten machst du dir Notizen (► *Listening*, p. 80).

2. Wenn es sich um einen Lesetext handelt, lies ihn jetzt ein weiteres Mal, Satz für Satz. Wenn du mit einer Kopie arbeitest, markiere die wichtigsten Passagen (► *Marking up texts*, p. 81). Denke dabei an die **5 Ws** – Textstellen, die auf solche Fragen wie die im Kasten antworten, sind wichtig!

3. Notiere nun alles, was du als wichtig markiert hast, in Stichpunkten auf einem separaten Blatt Papier. Überprüfe noch einmal, ob du wirklich alles Unnötige weggelassen hast.

4. Schreibe jetzt mit deinen eigenen Worten einen neuen Text. Bringe alles in eine logische Reihenfolge. Wenn du <u>fiktionale</u> Texte (Kurzgeschichten, Romane, …) zusammenfasst, verwende das **simple present** – auch wenn die Geschichte in der Vergangenheit spielt.
(► *Text types: fiction and non-fiction*, p. 83)
Im Hauptteil solltest du die wichtigsten Ereignisse einer Geschichte oder die Hauptpunkte eines Artikels wiedergeben. Greife dafür auf deine Notizen zu den **5 Ws** zurück. Schreib den Text nicht ab, sondern schreib auch hier wieder in eigenen Worten.

5. Überprüfe deinen Entwurf noch einmal. Enthält dein Text wirklich die wichtigsten Gedanken, Ereignisse, Ideen aus dem Original? Achte auch auf sprachliche Fehler.
(► *Checking and correcting your text*, p. 88)

6. Wenn dein Lehrer/deine Lehrerin eine bestimmte Anzahl von Wörtern für die *summary* vorgegeben hat, dann achte unbedingt darauf, diese Zahl einzuhalten. Wenn keine Zahl vorgegeben ist, sollte dein Text etwa ein Viertel bis ein Drittel so lang sein wie das Original.

7. Bringe den korrigierten Entwurf in eine Reinschrift.

Who?	Who does …?
	Who is the … about?
What?	What happens?
	What does he/she do?
When?	When does it take place?
Where?	Where does it take place?
Why?	Why does he/she act in this way?

The story is about …
The text describes / deals with …
The article shows …
In the story we get to know …

Check…

- Rechtschreibung
- Verwendung des *simple present* (bei *summaries* von fiktionalen Texten)
- Wortstellung
- Satzübergänge (*linking words:* **and, so, that's why, but, because, …**)

Schreib eine Zusammenfassung des Textes über Anna Perera (70–80 Wörter).

Anna Perera, children's writer

Anna Perera grew up just a few miles outside London, the city of her birth. Her mother was a Catholic, her father a Buddhist. And Anna herself? Well, she was mainly a bookworm. Like many of us, she discovered early in life that books were a passport out of this world into a world you could choose for yourself. One thing made her sad: the fact that no day was ever long enough to do all the reading she wanted.
Reading led to writing, although she had to wait a bit for success as an author. For a while, she worked as an English teacher at a number of London schools.

In her spare time she read and read. But that wasn't all. Visiting family, meeting friends and wearing nice clothes were fun too, she had discovered. So were music, dogs and horses … and flying, preferably in hot-air balloons.
Anna has heroes, too: people with a passion to discover new things. And she has dreams: a world in which people are kind to each other in little ways, day by day.
Her latest book is the story of a young English Muslim who is imprisoned in Guantanamo Bay. 15-year-old Khalid is abducted while visiting relatives in Pakistan. Anna tells a moving story of stolen childhood, stolen dreams, stolen hopes. (223 words)

14 Writing letters 4: 4

Beim Briefeschreiben musst du unterschiedliche Regeln beachten, je nachdem, ob du einen **förmlichen Brief** *(formal letter)* an eine Behörde, eine Firma oder eine Zeitschrift oder aber einen **persönlichen, informellen Brief** *(informal letter)* an Freunde oder Verwandte schreibst.

Formal letters

(1) Schreibe deine Adresse (ohne Namen!) und das Datum in die rechte obere Ecke. Verwende keine typisch deutschen Buchstaben wie ß, ä, ö oder ü.

(2) Die Anschrift steht links (wieder ohne Namen!).

(3) Die Anrede lautet ***Dear Sir or Madam***.
Wenn du den Namen des Adressaten kennst,
beginne deinen Brief mit ***Dear Mr/Mrs/Ms …***

(4) Benutze Langformen (*I am, I would like* statt *I'm, I'd like* usw.).

(5) Nenne zu Beginn den Grund deines Briefes.

(6) Wenn du Bitten oder Anfragen verschickst, bedanke dich im Voraus (*I look forward to hearing from you. Thank you.*).

(7) Beende den Brief mit ***Yours faithfully***, wenn du den Adressaten <u>nicht</u> kennst.
Hast du den Adressaten am Anfang des Briefes mit Namen angeredet, dann verwende ***Yours sincerely***.

(8) Unterschreibe den Brief. Tippe zusätzlich deinen Namen unter die Unterschrift.

---

(1) Waldstr. 5
50933 Koeln
Germany

(2) 1532 Beachview Place   20 May 2009
Los Angeles, CA
94832 - 1384
USA

(3) Dear Sir or Madam
(4) I am writing to you because I am really interested in (5) an article I read in your newspaper (May 2009). The title of the article is "New World, New Hopes, and New Problems" and it is about three immigrant families living in America. I have some questions, and I hope that you will be able to answer them.

I know that a lot of Americans are proud of their country. What about people who live in America but were not born there? Have you asked the families from the article how they feel about America? I would really like to know what they think.   (4)

I look forward to hearing from you soon. Thank you (6) very much.

(7) Yours faithfully
(8) *Tom Winter*
Tom Winter

Informal letters

Die Regeln für persönliche Briefe sind nicht ganz so streng:

- Schreibe deine Adresse (ohne Namen) und das Datum in die rechte obere Ecke.
- Verwende keine typisch deutschen Buchstaben wie ß, ä, ö, ü.
- Du benötigst keine Anschrift.
- Du kannst deinen Brief mit ***Dear … / Hello … / Hi …*** beginnen.
- Nenne zu Beginn den Grund für deinen Brief.
- Beende den Brief mit einem freundlichen Gruß, gefolgt von ***Love … / Lots of love … / Best wishes …*** oder ***All the best …***

Im Heidkampe 134
30659 Hanover

6 March 2009

Dear Mrs Henderson,
I've just arrived back in Hanover, and I wanted to thank you again for being a super hostess during my stay in Pontefract. I really enjoyed my time in Yorkshire, and I'll never forget the fantastic day trip to Liverpool. I took some really nice photos of the Cathedral – if you like, I can mail them to you. The flight back home was fine, and Dad was at Hanover airport to meet me. Thanks again for everything.
Best wishes,
Antonia Winkler

Sortiere die Ausdrücke aus dem blauen Kasten unten in eine Kopie dieser Tabelle ein.

	förmlicher Brief	persönlicher Brief
Beginn	Dear Mrs Jones, …	Dear Grandma, …
Ende	…	…

Best wishes • Dear Grandma • I look forward to hearing from you •
Yours faithfully • Dear Mrs Jones • Yours sincerely • Lots of love •
I look forward to meeting you. • Love • Dear Sir or Madam • See you soon! •
Hello Sarah • Happy birthday! • Hi • All the best

15 Writing course – SUMMARY (Schreibkurs – Zusammenfassung)

> ### The steps of writing
>
> 1. *Brainstorming* – Ideen sammeln und ordnen (▶ *Brainstorming*, p. 84)
>
> 2. **Schreiben**:
> – Texte gut strukturieren (▶ *Using paragraphs*, p. 87)
> – Sätze verbinden und ausbauen (▶ *Writing better sentences*, p. 87)
> – bei **Berichten**: *simple past* – bei **Zusammenfassungen**: *simple present*;
>   bei **Berichten** und **Zusammenfassungen**: die 5 Ws abdecken
>   (▶ *Writing reports*, p. 87 / *Writing summaries*, p. 85)
> – bei förmlichen Briefen: höfliche Anrede und Schlussformel verwenden
>   (▶ *Writing letters*, p. 86)
>
> 3. **Verbessern** – Texte inhaltlich und sprachlich überprüfen und korrigieren
>   (▶ *Checking and correcting your text*, p. 88)

Using paragraphs

Bei guten Texten lassen sich drei **Hauptabschnitte** erkennen:
– eine **Einleitung**, die in das Thema einführt
– ein **Hauptteil** (meist aus mehr als einem Absatz bestehend)
– ein **Schluss**, der den Text mit einer Zusammenfassung oder mit etwas Persönlichem zu einem interessanten Ende bringt.

Texte sind leichter zu lesen und zu verstehen, wenn sie in einzelne
Absätze *(paragraphs)* untergliedert sind:
– Neue inhaltliche Aspekte sollten mit einem neuen Absatz begonnen werden.
– Wenn ein Text aus sehr vielen Absätzen besteht, ist es hilfreich, wenn jeder
  Absatz mit einem **kurzen, einleitenden Satz** *(topic sentence)* beginnt.

Writing better sentences

Mit Konjunktionen, Relativpronomen und Zeitangaben kannst du
deine Sätze verbinden und deine Aussagen präziser formulieren:
– *Konjunktionen:* **although, and, because, but, so that,
                    that, when, while, ...**
– *Relativpronomen:* **who, which, that, whose**
– *Time phrases:*   **a few minutes later, suddenly, then, next,
                    at 7 o'clock, every morning, in the afternoons, ...**

> **!** Vorsicht bei <u>beschreibenden</u> Texten:
> – **Adjektive** beschreiben Personen,
>   Orte, Gegenstände, Erlebnisse:
>   a **careful** driver.
> – **Adverbien der Art und Weise**
>   beschreiben, wie (auf welche Art
>   und Weise) jemand etwas tut:
>   Drive **carefully**.

Writing reports

Achte bei **Berichten** auf Folgendes:
– Gib dem Leser eine **schnelle Orientierung**, was passiert ist.
– Beginne mit **wichtigen Informationen** und gib erst dann Detailinformationen.
– Gib Antworten auf die **5 Ws**: Who? What? When? Where? Why?
  Manchmal ist auch das How? wichtig.
– Verwende das *simple past*.
(▶ *Writing summaries*, p. 85)

(Fortsetzung ▶ p. 88)

Checking and correcting your text

Lies jeden Text, den du geschrieben hast, mehrmals durch:
– einmal, um zu sehen, ob er **vollständig** und **gut verständlich** ist,
– noch einmal, um ihn auf **Fehler** zu überprüfen.

■ **Rechtschreibfehler** *(Spelling mistakes)*
Lies deinen Text langsam, Wort für Wort, Buchstabe für Buchstabe.
Wenn du unsicher bist, schau in einem Wörterbuch nach.
Einige *spelling mistakes* kannst du vermeiden, wenn du die Tipps im Kasten rechts beachtest.

■ **Grammatikfehler** *(Grammar mistakes)*
Die Tipps rechts helfen dir, einige typische *grammar mistakes* zu vermeiden.
Der **Grammatik**-Teil dieses Heftes kann dir bei anderen Grammatikfragen weiterhelfen.
(▶ Inhaltsverzeichnis, S. 4–5 / Register, S. 95–97)

Der folgende Text ist völlig durcheinandergeraten, und er enthält 13 Fehler.

1 *Bringe den Text in eine für dich sinnvolle Reihenfolge.*

2 *Korrigiere alle spelling und grammar mistakes.*

3 *Unterstreiche in jedem Absatz den topic sentence.*

Spelling

Einige Wörter haben Buchstaben, die geschrieben, aber nicht gesprochen werden: <u>k</u>nife, autum<u>n</u>, clim<u>b</u>.

Manchmal ändert sich die Schreibung, wenn eine Endung hinzukommt: **run + ing → ru<u>nn</u>ing**; **drop + ed → dropped**, **make + ing → making**; **terribl<u>e</u> + ly → terribly**, **lucky + ly → luck<u>i</u>ly**; **try + s → tr<u>i</u>es**. **(aber: stay + s → stays)**.

Beim Plural tritt manchmal nicht nur **-s** hinzu, sondern **-es**: **church → churches**; **potato → potatoes**.

Grammar

Im *simple present* wird in der **3. Person Singular -s** (manchmal **-es**) angehängt: **he/she/it runs**; **he/she/it watc<u>h</u>es**

Manche Verben haben **unregelmäßige** *simple past-* und *past participle*-Formen: **go – went – gone**; **tell – told – told** (▶ *Irregular verbs*, pp. 67–68)

Verneinung: Im *simple present* werden Vollverben mit **don't/doesn't** verneint, im *simple past* mit **didn't**. (▶ *Simple present*, p. 15 / *Simple past*, p. 19)

Wortstellung: Die wichtigste Wortstellungsregel lautet **S**ubject – **V**erb – **O**bject. Sie gilt auch in Nebensätzen:
... when he saw my sister. ... als er meine Schwester sah.
Beachte, dass **verb** und **object** **nie** getrennt werden dürfen:
Dan has laid the table. Dan hat den Tisch gedeckt.
Sue <u>often</u> **plays** football. **Sue spielt** <u>oft</u> Fußball.
(▶ *Word order*, pp. 6–10)

How Daniel wrote his report

Finally he checkt and corrected his text.

Last week Daniel had to write a report about a class trip to the King Center.

He red it again twice and added two more adjectives and one time phrase.

He also founded two spelling mistakes.

He wrote about the center itself, the people who work their, and the things you can do there.

Then he typed it up nice.

When he had read his report one last time, he was quiet happy with the result.

For him, the writing of a report was easy because he knew the rules.

He starts by turning his notes into compleat sentences, and he made sure that he started a new paragraf with each new idea.

There was a lot to tell, so the mane part of his report had three paraghraphs.

He put all the material he had colected at the center on his desk and made notes on everything he wanted to write about.

Befor he started writing, he structured his notes.

Mediation skills

16 Mediation

Was ist „Mediation"?

Manchmal musst du zwischen zwei Sprachen vermitteln, z.B. wenn Sprecher verschiedener Sprachen aufeinandertreffen. Das nennt man **Mediation** (oder **Vermittlung**, manchmal auch **Sprachmittlung**).

1. Du gibst **englische Informationen auf Deutsch** wieder,
   z.B. wenn du in einem englischsprachigen Land bist, und jemand möchte wissen, was gesagt wurde oder was auf einer Informationstafel steht.

2. Du gibst **deutsche Informationen auf Englisch** wieder,
   z.B. wenn jemand kein Deutsch spricht und Hilfe braucht.

3. In schriftlichen Prüfungen musst du manchmal in einem englischen Text gezielt nach Informationen suchen und diese auf Deutsch wiedergeben. Oder du sollst Informationen aus einem deutschen Text auf Englisch wiedergeben.

> Entschuldigung, kannst du mir mal helfen? Mein Englisch ist nicht so gut.

> Excuse me, she's looking for a shop where they sell aspirin.

> ... Apotheke ...?

Worauf muss ich achten?

– Übersetze nicht alles wörtlich, sondern gib nur das Wesentliche wieder.
– Du kannst Sätze auch umformulieren.
– Verwende möglichst kurze und einfache Sätze.

Was kann ich tun, wenn ich ein wichtiges Wort nicht kenne?

Manchmal ist es gar nicht so einfach, zwischen zwei Sprachen zu vermitteln, z.B.
– wenn dein Wortschatz nicht ausreicht,
– wenn dir bekannte Wörter „im Stress" nicht einfallen,
– wenn spezielle Fachbegriffe auftauchen.

Dann musst du versuchen, die „schwierigen" Wörter zu umschreiben.
Dabei sind **Relativsätze** eine große Hilfe.
(▸ *Paraphrasing*, p. 84 / ▸ *Relative clauses*, pp. 59–61)

> It's somebody/a person who ...
> It's something that you use to ...
> It's an animal that ...
> It'a place that/where ...

1 Dein kleiner Bruder hat ein funkferngesteu-
ertes Auto bekommen, aber die Beschreibung
ist nur auf Englisch. Kannst du ihm erklären,
worum es hier geht?

> Be sure nobody else is using the same
> frequency. Using the same frequency at
> the same time can cause loss of control
> and lead to serious accidents. Apply
> frequency sticker to vehicle antenna to
> show frequency being used.
> Racing in groups is possible only if
> different frequencies are used.

2 Die Band Silbermond *gibt ein Konzert in eurer Nähe. Eure
amerikanische Austauschschülerin hat folgenden Text
über die Band gefunden und bittet dich um Hilfe.*

> *Silbermond* gingen aus der Band *Exakt* hervor, die 1998
> von Mitgliedern des Jugendprojekts *Ten Sing* gegründet
> wurde. Zunächst spielten sie überwiegend Coversongs.
> Erste eigene, deutschsprachige Songs entstanden 2001.
> Ihr drittes Album erschien 2009 und belegte sofort
> Platz 1 der Charts. *Silbermond* verstehen sich als
> Rockband. Obwohl sie als Singles meist Balladen ver-
> öffentlichten, besteht ihr Repertoire hauptsächlich aus
> schnellen, oft instrumental geprägten Titeln.

Exam skills

17 Tests and exams (Tests und Prüfungen) 4:1 / 4:4

Countdown zum Testerfolg

Ein Test ist angekündigt? Wenn du weißt, worauf du dich vorbereiten musst, gibt es keinen Grund zur Panik! Im Zweifelsfall frag deine Lehrerin oder deinen Lehrer. Und dann kann der Countdown beginnen!

■ **Eine Woche vor dem Test**

1. Lies noch einmal die **Texte** der zuletzt durchgenommenen Unit (vor allem *Lead-in*, *A-Section* und *Text*, eventuell auch das *Background File*).
   Fasse mündlich oder schriftlich zusammen, worum es ging.

2. Wiederhole den **Wortschatz** der Unit mit Hilfe des *Vocabulary*, des *Wordmaster* oder des *English Coach*. Schreib die Wörter und Wendungen, die du immer wieder vergisst, auf ein Blatt Papier. Mindmaps und Wortfelder helfen beim Behalten.

3. Geh auch noch mal die neue **Grammatik** durch. Aufgaben zur Selbstüberprüfung und zum Üben findest du in deinem Englischbuch (im *Practice*-Teil, auf den *How am I doing?*-Seiten, im *Grammar File*), in deinem *Workbook* und im *e-Workbook*. Grammatische Regeln kannst du im *Grammar File* deines Englischbuchs oder im Grammatik-Teil dieses Heftes nachlesen.

■ **Zwei oder drei Tage vor dem Test**

1. Wiederhole den **Wortschatz**. Manche Wörter „sitzen" noch nicht? Schreibe einen kurzen Text, in dem du sie verwendest.

2. Lies die Unit-**Texte** (und die Stichpunkte, die du dir dazu notiert hast) ein weiteres Mal. Erzähle einem Freund/einer Freundin, worum es geht.

3. Erkläre einem Freund oder einer Freundin die neue **Grammatik**.
   Lies bei Bedarf im *Grammar File* oder im Grammatik-Teil dieses Heftes nach.

■ **Am Abend vor dem Test**

1. Entspann dich. Lies, leg dich in die Badewanne, hör Musik, sieh fern, …

2. Geh zur gewohnten Zeit ins Bett.

■ **Am Morgen des Tests**

1. Steh rechtzeitig auf, damit du nicht hetzen musst.

2. Lies etwas „zum Aufwärmen", aber schau nicht mehr in dein Schülerbuch.

■ **Während des Tests**

1. Denk daran: Du hast dich gut vorbereitet. Es gibt keinen Grund, nervös zu sein.

2. Konzentriere dich auf den Test, lass dich nicht ablenken.

3. Lies dir die Aufgaben genau durch. Dann löse zuerst die Aufgaben, die dir einfach scheinen. Wende dich erst danach den schwereren Aufgaben zu.

4. Aufgaben, die du bearbeitet hast, hakst du ab. So siehst du, wie du vorankommst, und behältst den Überblick.

5. Schau ab und zu auf die Uhr. Du solltest etwas Zeit einplanen, um deine Antworten noch einmal durchlesen und wenn nötig korrigieren zu können.

Aufgabenstellungen verstehen

Überlege, ob du wirklich genau verstanden hast, was du tun sollst,
bevor du anfängst, die Aufgaben zu bearbeiten!
Lies die Aufgabenstellung Wort für Wort langsam und gründlich und von
Anfang bis Ende durch. Unterstreiche besonders wichtige Teile und unterteile,
wenn nötig, die Aufgabe für dich in einzelne Schritte.

Und bei Multiple-Choice-Aufgaben ...

– Lies die Frage oder die Aussage sehr genau durch.
– Deck die zur Wahl stehenden Lösungen zunächst mit Papier ab und überlege,
  wie die richtige Antwort lauten könnte. Ist deine Antwort unter den angebotenen Lösungsmöglichkeiten? Dann ist sie wahrscheinlich richtig.
– Lies aber trotzdem erst alle angebotenen Lösungen, bevor du dich
  entscheidest.
– Kreuze nur eine Antwort an, es sei denn, dass ausdrücklich gesagt wird, dass
  mehrere Antworten richtig sein können.
– Bearbeite auf diese Weise alle Multiple-Choice-Aufgaben so gut du kannst,
  ohne etwas auszulassen. Geh am Ende zu den Fragen zurück, bei denen du
  unsicher warst.
– Wenn du die richtige Antwort nicht findest, dann suche nach den falschen
  Antworten! Manchmal ist es einfacher zu entscheiden, welche Antworten
  falsch sind. Auf diese Weise kannst du erschließen, welche Antwort richtig ist.

Die folgenden Aufgaben beziehen sich auf den gesamten Skills-Teil dieses Heftes.
Wenn du die Antwort nicht weißt, überlege erst, wo du nachschlagen könntest.
(Das Inhaltsverzeichnis auf S. 74 hilft dir zu finden, was du suchst.)
Manchmal gibt es mehr als eine richtige Lösung.

1 Wenn ich mit einem zweisprachigen Wörterbuch arbeite, ...
  A schaue ich mir den gesamten Eintrag zu „meinem" Wort an.
  B nehme ich immer die erste Übersetzung, die mir angeboten wird.
  C achte ich darauf, dass ich bei der richtigen Wortart nachschlage.

2 Einsprachige Wörterbücher helfen, ...
  A Wörter und Wendungen richtig zu verwenden.
  B Wörter und Wendungen richtig zu schreiben und auszusprechen.
  C richtige Übersetzungen zu finden.

3 Was ist korrekt?
  A *skimming = reading for detail*   **B** *scanning = drawing conclusions*   **C** *scanning = looking for key words*

4 Was ist korrekt?
  A *characters* = die Personen in einem fiktionalen Text
  B *narrator* = die Hauptperson in einem fiktionalen Text
  C *setting* = Ort, Zeit und Umstände der Handlung

5 Einen *formal letter* beginne ich mit ...
  A *Dear Sir or Madam*   **B** *Dear Mr Smith*   **C** *Dear Claire*

6 Was ist korrekt?
  A *although* = also   **B** *while* = weil   **C** *when* = als

7 Bei der Mediation ...
  A muss ich möglichst genau den Originaltext wiedergeben.
  B kann ich unbekannte Wörter und Wendungen umschreiben.
  C muss ich nur das Wichtigste wiedergeben.

Lösungen

Bei vielen Aufgaben gibt es nicht nur eine einzige korrekte Lösung (z.B. bei den Aufgaben zu den Kapiteln Outlines *oder* Handouts*). Wenn deine Lösung bei solchen Aufgaben sehr stark von den hier vorge-schlagenen Lösungen abweicht, dann bitte deinen Lehrer/deine Lehrerin, deine Lösung anzuschauen.*

p.75 1 Working with dictionaries
a) Wem wurde der erste Preis verliehen?
b) Sie konnten die Krise nicht abwenden.
c) Der Lärm/Das Geräusch hielt ihn die ganze Nacht wach.
d) Glücklicherweise konnte der Fahrer dem Hund ausweichen.
e) Not pizza again! – Then what? / What then?
f) We're working on it.
g) You shouldn't wait for it.
h) I'm proud of it.

p.76 1 Working with dictionaries
1 a) **critic** *Kritiker/in* – **criticism** *Kritik*
  b) **lift** *(BE)* – **elevator** *(AE)*
  c) (to) **sew** [səʊ], **sewed**, **sewn**
2 a) (to) **be good at sth.**
  b) (to) **play a trick on sb.**
  c) (to) **have an experience**
  d) (to) **be popular with sb.**

p.76 2 Describing and analysing pictures
(Description) The photo shows three girls and a boy in a classroom. In the foreground there is a desk and two chairs. On the right, one of the girls is sitting on another desk. The other two girls are standing next to her, one to her right, one to her left. The girl on the desk has a music magazine in her hands, and the girls are all looking at it. They are smiling.
The boy is on the left of the photo. He is also sitting on a desk, with his left foot on one of the chairs in the foreground. He is also looking at a magazine, but he is not smiling.
In the background, on the left, there is a board on a blue wall. The other wall, on the right of the photo, is white, and there are some posters on it.
(Analysis) The girls look as if they are having fun. Maybe they have just read a funny story, or they are looking at some funny pictures or cartoons. Maybe the boy feels a bit left out because the girls are not talking to him. Or he is thinking about what he has just read or seen in his magazine.

p.77 3 Outlines
Schools in the USA
I Types of school
   A. Facts and figures
   B. Two examples
II A typical school day
   A. The school bus
   B. A class schedule
   C. Extracurricular activities
III Differences USA – Germany
   A. School grades
   B. School subjects

p.78 4 Research
a) Man **kann** lange Zitate ungekürzt stehen lassen, darf sie aber auch kürzen, denn lange Zitate können ermüdend wirken und den Eindruck erwecken, dass der/die Vortragende selbst nichts zu sagen hat.
b) Falsch – man sollte Informationen zunächst speichern und bearbeiten und dann ausdrucken, was wirklich wichtig ist.
c) Richtig.
d) Falsch – Quellen müssen immer angegeben werden; bei Internetseiten auch Datum und Uhrzeit des letzten Zugriffs.
e) Richtig.
f) Richtig.
g) Falsch – man muss nicht wörtlich zitieren, aber wenn man eigene Formulierungen verwendet, muss man trotzdem Autor und Quelle angeben (in diesem Fall verwendet man keine Anführungszeichen, sondern setzt das Wort „vgl." vor Autoren- und Quellenangabe).
h) Richtig.

p.79 6 Handouts
Eine gute Präsentation
Vorbereitung
1) Stichpunkte machen; ordnen (Karteikarten; Mindmap)
2) Material vorbereiten (Folien, Poster, Handout)
3) Üben
Durchführung
1) Unterlagen und Medien sortieren; Technik überprüfen
2) Thema nennen
3) Frei und langsam sprechen; Blickkontakt
4) Unbekannte Wörter anschreiben
Schluss
1) Fragen zum Thema?
2) Bedanken

p.81 8/9 Marking up texts / Taking notes

Twilight is a love story about 17-year-old Bella and Edward, a boy with dreamy good looks who, Bella learns, is really a vampire. But this is no ordinary vampire story – it's a book in a class of its own which readers of all ages will definitely enjoy.

The story is told by Bella, and because she is the narrator we don't learn directly how the other characters feel or think. This increases the suspense. At first we know only a little about Edward and his family, but as the story develops we slowly get a bigger picture of these outsiders. Our appetite for more grows. What makes the story even more readable is that Bella is a very credible character, shy and without much self-confidence, but very likeable nevertheless.

Twilight is extremely well written, in language that is easy to understand. When you read about Forks, the town where the story is set, you feel as if you are there, walking through the permanent mist and rain.

A romance like this will move even the toughest of readers to tears. You won't put the book down until you have turned the very last page. Can the love between the two heroes survive? Will the two lovers themselves survive? Buy the book and find out.

Notizen:

What?	love story
Who?	Bella and Edward (vampire!)
	Bella = narrator –> suspense
	Bella: credible character; likeable, shy
Where?	Forks (town; mist and rain)
Why?	language easy to understand; will move readers to tears; won't stop reading

p.83 10 Reading course: Drawing conclusions

1 Children that have to work on farms; "Kinderarbeit" (engl.: *child labour*)

2 In northern Mexico, many young children work in the fields. They only earn seven dollars a day. Some of them can go to school after work, but only for a few hours.

3 Children like J. don't have a real childhood, they don't have time to play with other children. They don't get a good education because they only go to school for two to three hours/because their job keeps them from school.
They probably won't get a good job later because they don't have a good education.

p.83 10 Reading course: Text types

Text 1:

1 Latisha, Anna, Latisha's mother

2 Latisha's home; Friday afternoon

3 Latisha is the first-person narrator.

Text 2:

1 Katrina, the film crew, Bill, the captain, passengers

2 the ferry to Hoy, Lyness; Friday morning

3 The narrator is not a character in the story.

p.84 11 Paraphrasing

a) **Pfütze** – water that you find in the street when there has been a lot of rain; little kids like to put their feet in them

b) **Balkon** – flats sometimes have one; you can go outside and look down on the street from them; some people grow flowers on them

c) **Spargel** – a vegetable; it is usually white or green and looks a bit like a long candle; you can buy it in May and June in Germany

d) **a caravan** – a small house with two wheels; you can take it with you in your holidays, e.g. when you go camping and don't want to sleep in tents

e) **a paddle** – you use it to make a small boat – for example a canoe – move forwards through the water; it is usually made of wood or plastic

f) **cloudy** – when it's cloudy, you can't see the sun, and you might get rain

p.84 12 Brainstorming

1 **Planning a party:** (1) talk to parents, (2) invite friends, (3) ask friends for help, (4–6) buy food/drinks/decoration, (7) make cake, (8) look for good music, (9) prepare room

2 **Vampirgeschichte:** *individuelle Lösungen*

p.85 13 Writing summaries

Anna Perera grew up near London. As a child she liked reading a lot because she discovered her own new worlds in her books. Later she started writing and she also worked as an English teacher. Among her many hobbies, reading has always been her favourite. Anna's heroes are people who like to discover something new – like Khaled, the hero of her latest novel. He is a Muslim boy who is a prisoner at Guantanamo Bay.

(Hinweis: Es handelt sich um einen nicht-fiktionalen Text, daher die Verwendung des simple past *in der* summary.)

p.86 **14** Writing letters

Förmlicher Brief:

Beginn: Dear Mrs Jones – Dear Sir or Madam

Ende: I look forward to hearing from you/to meeting you – Yours faithfully – Yours sincerely

Persönlicher Brief:

Beginn: Dear Grandma – Hello Sarah – Hi

Ende: Best wishes – Lots of love – Love – See you soon! – Happy birthday! – All the best

p.88 **15** Writing course

How Daniel wrote his report

Last week Daniel had to write a report about a class trip to the King Center. He put all the material he had collected at the center on his desk and made notes on everything he wanted to write about. Before he started writing, he structured his notes.

For him, the writing of a report was easy because he knew the rules. He started by turning his notes into complete sentences, and he made sure that he started a new paragraph with each new idea. There was a lot to tell, so the main part of his report had three paragraphs. He wrote about the center itself, the people who work there, and the things you can do there.

Finally he checked and corrected his text. He read it again twice and added two more adjectives and one time phrase. He also found two spelling mistakes. Then he typed it up nicely. When he had read his report one last time, he was quite happy with the result.

p.89 **16** Mediation

1 Hier steht, dass du darauf achten musst, dass niemand dieselbe Frequenz benutzt wie du – du könntest sonst die Kontrolle über das Auto verlieren und es könnte Unfälle geben. Du sollst den Aufkleber mit der Frequenzangabe an der Antenne des Autos befestigen, sodass man sehen kann, welche Frequenz du benutzt. Rennen in Gruppen können nur gefahren werden, wenn unterschiedliche Frequenzen benutzt werden.

2 The band *Silbermond* developed out of the band *Exact,* founded by members of a youth project in 1988. They only played cover versions at first and started writing their own songs – with German lyrics – in 2001. Their third album was released in 2009. It went straight to number 1 in the charts. *Silbermond* see themselves as a rock band. They have released a couple of ballads, but most of their songs are fast, with lots of instrumental parts.

p.91 **17** Tests and exams

1) **A** **C**

2) **A** **B**

3) **C**

4) **A** **C**

5) **A** **B**

6) **C**

7) **B** **C**

Register (Index)

Die Ziffern bezeichnen die **Abschnitte des *Grammar*-Teils** (nicht die Seitenzahlen).
Beispiel: *a lot of* 36.1 → Zu *a lot of* findest du etwas im Abschnitt 36.1.
(**K**= Kontrast-Abschnitt, **!**= Abschnitt mit Warnsymbol)